die
with
your
helmet
on

dr. tom olson

the power of personal responsibility

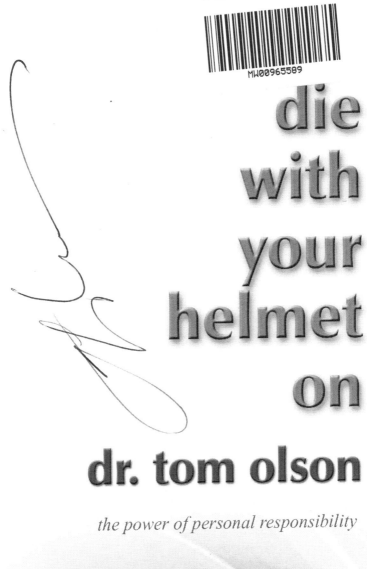

Previous CIP data: BF637.S4O48 2004 158.1   C2004-903605-X

For more information or to order additional copies, please contact:
Tom Olson, PhD 103 Silverthorn Way NW
Calgary, AB, T3B 4K2
1-888-884-2020
www.onebookbookstore.com

Layout and cover design, Nadien Cole Advertising, Calgary, Alberta

Note for Librarians: A cataloguing record for this book is available from Library and Archives Canada at www.collectionscanada.ca/amicus/index-e.html
ISBN 1-4251-1216-1

Printed in Victoria, BC, Canada. Printed on paper with minimum 30% recycled fibre.
Trafford's print shop runs on "green energy" from solar, wind and other environmentally-friendly power sources.

Offices in Canada, USA, Ireland and UK

Book sales for North America and international:
Trafford Publishing, 6E–2333 Government St.,
Victoria, BC V8T 4P4 CANADA
phone 250 383 6864 (toll-free 1 888 232 4444)
fax 250 383 6804; email to orders@trafford.com
Book sales in Europe:
Trafford Publishing (UK) Limited, 9 Park End Street, 2nd Floor
Oxford, UK OX1 1HH UNITED KINGDOM
phone +44 (0)1865 722 113 (local rate 0845 230 9601)
facsimile +44 (0)1865 722 868; info.uk@trafford.com
Order online at:
trafford.com/06-2975

10 9 8 7 6 5 4 3 2 1

dedication

This little book is dedicated
to the memory of my great friend,
James Douglas Staples—
who, to paraphrase Ralph Waldo Emerson,
Laughed often and much;
won the respect of intelligent people
and the affection of children;
earned the appreciation of honest critics
and endured the betrayal of false friends;
appreciated beauty and found the best in others;
and left the world a little better
by his children, his work,
and a redeemed social condition.
We've all breathed easier because you lived;
you, my friend, were a great success.
Here's lookin' at you, pal.

and

to my lovely wife, Marce,
without whom I would never have completed this—
after all these years,
still the best human being I know.

Tom Olson

table of contents

Tom Olson

introduction

As a professional speaker and trainer, I'm often asked about the availability of my books, tapes,   or videos. "Don't have any," I say. "I've been too busy training and speaking to write, but I do plan to get around to it someday."

Well, someday arrived, and I had to make good on that promise. I'd been making noises about writing something for so long that someone (it could have been my wife) finally challenged me to *do it*. I think the exact words were something like "put up or shut up"! And because I thought writing would be easier than not talking, I made my way to the keyboard, sketched out some ideas, and began converting thoughts to words. I now wish I'd done it years ago—it's been fun and, immodest as it may sound, I actually *like* what's come out!

This is not a book in the traditional sense; rather, it's a collection of essays on topics that inspired the greatest interest and/or response in my training or speaking sessions. What are these about? Well, the unifying theme is best described by this quote from a 1910 speech Theodore Roosevelt gave at the Sorbonne:

It is not the critic who counts, not the man who points out how the strong man stumbles or where the doer of deeds could have done them better. The credit belongs to the man who is actually in the arena, whose face is marred by dust and sweat and blood, who strives valiantly, who errs and comes short again and again because there is no effort without error and shortcomings, who knows the great devotion, who spends himself in a worthy cause, who at best knows in the end the high achievement of triumph and who at worst, if he fails while daring greatly, knows his place shall never be with those timid and cold souls who know neither victory nor defeat.

Success is in the arena. My experience is that many people want to be in there—that our latter-day culture of entitlement, victimhood, and fear frustrates them, and they would like to take more responsibility for the events taking place in and around their lives.

So, it is those for whom I've written this collection. Although I don't expect those in the psychological or psychiatric community to read this book, should it fall into the hands of a professional from one of these groups I expect it will be received poorly. Why? Because the lessons of this book are taught not by professionals or always supported by mountains of academic research. Rather, they are based on the experiences of successful people I have had the pleasure of knowing throughout my life—people from all walks of life, who have achieved great things, and through words and deeds have taught others to do the same.

The essays are anything but academic in nature. They are quite personal, journalistic in style, and I hope eminently readable. Although there is a bit of a sequence, you can start with any one of them. They were all fun to write, but my favourite is the last one: "Weasel, Toad, Slippery, and Puke."

Apart from meeting the "put - up - or - shut - up" challenge, I had a few other reasons for putting this tome together. One, I thought it would give my children some insight into how I actually make a living. For years, the answer to the question, "What is it, again, that your father does?" has eluded them. I hope this will help.

And because I'm not altogether altruistic, I'd like to make a dollar or two from all this effort. To that end, we offer training: speaking and various audio-video products based on the book's content. If you're interested in any of this, please call me at 1-888-884-2020, and I'll be happy to provide you with the details. Or, if you prefer, please send a note through our Web site:

www.dontdiewithyourhelmeton.com

Of course, you can also order more books either through the Web site or by calling the toll-free number above. We do offer bulk discounts.

And just to let you know that I'm not a heartless mercenary, three charities—the Cancer Society, Samaritan's Purse, and the Heart and Stroke Foundation—will each receive a portion of the proceeds from this book and any of the products and services related to it.

Thanks!
Tom Olson
March 25, 2004

Tom Olson

Chapter One

don't die with your helmet on

*The people who get on in this world are
the people who get up and look for the
circumstances they want, and, if they
can't find them, make them.*

—George Bernard Shaw

The suit I was married in is now back in style, and my wife and I just opened our second bottle of Tabasco sauce. Our marriage has lasted that long—more than thirty years. Although it doesn't seem all that long to us, for many young people—some of whom can't understand how Britney Spears handled the pressures of being legally hooked up for almost *an entire day*—it's a feat of historical proportions.

"What's the secret?" they ask.

Now, I'm going to be upfront here. It doesn't matter what the question is—I love to be asked. It gives me a chance to furrow my brow, stroke my head, appear wise, and pontificate about life, money, the world, politics, sports, —you name it—I can dredge up an opinion on just about anything.

Unfortunately, I have a lot of trouble looking wise, am a very poor pontificator, and, if I stroke my head too often,

I'll simply rub off more of my hair. When I try to look wise, I'm more likely to be mistaken for Yoda with a bad case of stomach cramps than someone ready to reveal the secrets of life and the universe.

Oh, I'd love to have Yoda's wisdom, Brad Pitt's looks, Bill Gate's money, Condoleezza Rice's brains, Dave Barry's humour, Oprah's gift of relating to the masses, Grisham's knack for story telling, and the regal bearing of any prince except either Charles or the Artist Formally Known as.

In truth, I'm short on all of these qualities. I have more in common with people who are short, pudgy, growing a hole in their hair, raising their kids, living from paycheque to paycheque, drinking screw-top wine—you know: just plain folks.

Essentially, I'm a cracker-barrel philosopher putting my own spin on common-sense ideas and advice passed on to me by the many successful people with whom I've been lucky enough to work and play with over the years.

So when I'm asked the secret of a long marriage,* I stay away from the more esoteric stuff (most of which is plain hooey, anyway), and simply say, "I have no idea."

Maybe it's business travel. In our thirty-plus years, I've probably really only been home for five or six in total—maybe absence *does* make the heart grow fonder! I'm kidding, of course. One thing I *do* know, though, is that we talk with one another a lot—maybe that's what's kept us together.

For thirty-five years, my wife and I have talked each other's ears off (figuratively speaking, of course). We talk while we eat, we talk while we walk; we talk while on airplanes, buses, trains, and in the car. We talk in front of the fire, we talk in front of the television set; we talk in front of the kids, we talk in front of our friends, we talk in front of our relatives, we talk in front of strangers.

We talk about the important and the trivial, the religious and secular, politics and show business (I put these together because, as some wag said, politics is just show business for less-attractive people), children and grandchildren, sports and... (well, *I* talk about sports), the past and future—anything that strikes our fancy. I guess you could say that throughout the years, neither of us has ever shut up except to listen to the other. Talking and listening (listening, is of course the hard part—*maybe that's the secret!*)—that's how the idea and the title for this epistle came about—talking and listening.

As we were solving the problems of the world on one of our walk-and-talk sessions, the conversation turned to the subject of bicycle helmets. Why bicycle helmets, you ask? Well, on that very day, the government of British Columbia was preparing to legislate mandatory use of bicycle helmets. Regardless of age, gender, creed, colour, size, or the speed at which one pedaled, under law, if you got on a bike, you would have to wear a helmet.

My wife thought it was a good idea, given that a tumble from a fast-moving Schwinn can do some serious damage to the old melon. Because I'm a contrarian by nature (and because automatically agreeing with my wife about *anything* is *really* against my nature), I suggested the legislation was overkill—and besides, according to a newspaper article I had recently read, more people suffered head injuries *falling out of bed* than falling from bicycles! Because my logic is somewhat twisted at times, I suggested this finding implied one is at greater risk in bed than on a bike.

And the risk would increase if one did anything other than lie absolutely still—no movement whatsoever. And, the logical extension of this is (and you know where I'm going here) don't even think a lascivious thought—unless you're wearing a helmet! While not necessarily agreeing with me, just the thought of bed helmets got my wife's mind rolling!

Mandatory helmets in the bedroom—oh, the government jobs *that* would create! There'd need to be proper standards for helmets developed, consultation with the World Health Organization, government grants to help people with the costs of renovating bedrooms to accommodate helmet storage, and, of course, a *Helmet Registry* to make sure that helmets were locked safely in a helmet cabinet when not in use (chinstraps stored separately, of course).

We'd need Helmet Police—government drones responsible for investigating, apprehending and bringing to justice those who contravened the *"Don't even think of you know what without a helmet"* law.

It might cost a couple of million of taxpayers dollars to set it up but people would be safer-wouldn't they? And if the goal was to make people feel safer, didn't it make sense that people should wear helmets twenty-four-seven, regardless of the activity. That way nobody could ever be hurt!

Chopping vegetables—wear a helmet. Taking out the garbage—wear a helmet. Thinking about buying a new house—wear a helmet. The longer we walked and talked, the more apparent it became to us that we live in a world filled with figurative bicycle helmets. They come in different sizes and shapes, but are all designed to do the same thing—appeal to our need for security. We have government helmets, social helmets, religious helmets, occupational helmets, and personal helmets. Putting on a helmet makes us feel a little safer—a little more secure.

Great in theory—but security usually comes at the expense of freedom. The act of putting on a helmet limits our choices and affects our decisions. Take, for example, health care in Canada. The Canadian system of universal health care is, according to many in this country, the best in the world. For some, it is what distinguishes us from Americans and defines us as Canadians.

We're secure in the belief that quality health care will always be there at no cost when we need it. But we cannot choose between the public services offered and those made available by a private hospital. Even if the waiting time is shorter, or the quality of care offered by a private hospital is better, we are bound to the public system. (Of course, one can always leave the country to have a hip replaced or an MRI done in the United States, but that essentially means you're paying twice for the service—once in taxes, and again from your wallet.)

Universal health care is a big government helmet, but there are many others, mostly in the form of one regulation or another. The "best before date" message on food packaging, for example, is a small, government helmet. The government agencies and consumer advo-cates that foisted this bit of nonsense on us have in my mind contributed to the greatest marketing scam in history. "Use by" makes sense to me, but "best before"— I'm not sure.

When my daughters come to visit, the first thing they do is raid the refrigerator—not for something to eat, but to examine the food. They examine every tub of sour cream, carton of milk, package of bacon, and brick of ice cream, to make certain that none of it passed the dreaded "best before" date. They roll their eyes, sigh loudly, and mutter about their parents' lack of health consciousness as they separate the expired from that which is, in their minds, safe. And then, with great ceremony, they turf a whole bunch of perfectly good food. (What they don't know is that after they've gone, we put it all back.)

Now, I *will* admit that, on occasion, there are things in our fridge that resemble some other life form—usually something like a Tupperware container of leftover chili, or a piece of pizza that I intended to eat during the 1998 Stanley Cup Playoffs, but never found when I went looking for it.

My mother had her own "best before" system—she would sniff at anything left in the refrigerator and pronounce it "gone off" (which usually meant something like "it's starting to reproduce itself"), or say, "I think if we boil it, it'll be okay." But like so many others today, my daughters think—no, actually *believe*—that eating something twenty-five seconds past its "best before" date will immediately bring about the type of gastrointestinal upheaval usually associated with drinking water straight from the River Ganges, or even worse, the Victoria Harbour! It's simply not true! "Best before" means, simply, that!

I'd like to see some sort of graduated scale —best before August 22; a little less tasty up to October 6; beginning to smell and taste somewhat strange up to November 15; you're taking your life into your own hands until December 5, and, if you eat this *after* December 5, make sure your affairs are in order.

Best-before dates are suggestions, not rules. I shudder to think how much food we discard or waste because of how this little bit of government-inspired labeling is misunderstood. Do people in North Africa worry about best-before dates? I think not. While in Khartoum a few years ago, I ate breakfast cereal that had a best—before date in the early 1990s. This horrified my daughters when I told them. Much to their surprise, however, I lived to tell about it!

Will a food bank accept food beyond its best before date? I don't know.

It's annoying, but it's a minor helmet.

Oh, but there are so many more. The all too Canadian obsession with risk-avoidance has encouraged the design and manufacture of thousands of government helmets, and the creation of a Helmet Police who will ensure that you pay for not donning the government-approved and mandated headgear. To catalogue and comment on all of these would take years and, in all likelihood, cause my blood pressure to rise to dangerous levels, so we'll leave the government helmets for another time, and concentrate on those of our own design.

Social, religious, and occupational helmets are ones we design ourselves. Each provides us with a specific type of security, but at the same time limits what we can discuss and how we behave. The occupational helmet may be the most limiting of all.

I was once a public schoolteacher. Because of my background in education, over the years I have spoken at numerous educational meetings and conferences. Invariably, during the small group discussions that follow my presentations, many people will ask how they can get out of teaching and into the business of employee development and making presentations. (The number of teachers who would rather be doing something else would amaze you.) I understand why they ask, of course. I mean, who *wouldn't* want my job? I get to travel, I'm reasonably well paid, and the work certainly looks easy!

"Getting out of teaching is easy," I tell them. "Write a letter to the superintendent of schools that says 'I quit.'" This always causes more than a little discomfort. I then open my calendar to a page three months or so in the future—a page that is completely blank. I explain that a blank page means no bookings that day, week, or even month. No bookings equals no money. "If you can live with that," say I, "write the letter. If you can't, put your pen and paper away." I've never known anyone who has written the letter.

The situation is not exclusive to teachers—many of the people I talk to are frustrated, unhappy, and working for managers and supervisors they neither like nor respect. Their frustration is exacerbated by the fact that they enjoy very little control over the decisions that most affect their work lives—decisions about work assignments, mobility, salary, career advancement and so on. In a nutshell, many feel that they have no control.

Many people would prefer to be doing something else—chasing their dreams—but, in their minds, the risks are too great. Better to be less happy, but secure. Better to put dreams on hold, or let them die. They subscribe to the notion that "A bird in the hand is worth two in the bush."

I'm familiar with these notions, because I grew up with them. For many years, they were part of my paradigm. My father had struggled through the Depression, never out of work, but never having anything close to stability or a career.

As a result, his message to me was, "Look for security above all else. Get a good job—one with paid vacations, sick pay, a medical plan, and a good pension plan" (preferably with the government). And so, like a good son, I did just that—I became a teacher. I went to work each day, enjoying the students, but hating the system. I was tenured—secure, but unhappy, thinking less about where I could be and more about where I was. I began engaging in unhealthy and self-destructive behaviour. Lowering my expectations, I began counting the days until retirement. I had only been teaching for five years!

Thank God, an opportunity to quit presented itself. I had moved from classroom teaching to a job that required me to bring a rural school board and two com-munity groups together to accomplish a joint recreational/educational initiative. The school board held my contract and subcontracted my services to the two community groups. Long story made short: just over a year into the project, the community groups withdrew, leaving the school board on the hook for my salary.

Although the project had folded up, the school board was still obligated to pay me. To get value for their money, they decided to send me back into classroom teaching. The job involved teaching junior-high girls physical education and home economics—*absolutely the worst offer* I'd ever *been made!* I had no clue about physical education, and didn't know blancmange from a rutabaga!

With one child, a big mortgage on a new house, and no other prospects, what could I do? I needed the job, the money!

So I quit. I not only took off the security helmet, but I tossed it out the window.

I quit and went to work for someone who wouldn't fire me, transfer me, restrict my earnings, require me to take ridiculous assignments, play political games with me, or above all, squelch my ideas and ambitions. Someone who would encourage my intellect and make sure I had the opportunity to become better than I was. And who was that person? Well, the only person I knew who was willing to do all of that and more was... me.

To hire me, I had to trade what security I had for the freedom I needed—exactly the opposite of what I had been doing, and what most people usually do. People tend to trade the *freedom*—to pursue their dreams, maximize their talents, and control their own destiny—for *security.* The problem is that, often after that trade is made, dreams die and skills diminish, because one has given up control over those things that most inform, influence, and instruct one's life.

And, as many people have found out, the security they traded for is often illusory. Jobs can, have, and will quickly disappear with a downturn in the economy, a corporate restructuring, or at the whim of a new executive vice president.

According to author and speaker Mark Victor Hansen, in life there are two doors, one marked *security* and the other marked *freedom.* "If you choose security," he says, "you get neither."

I agree! And, in my view, feelings of freedom and success, job satisfaction and happiness are all directly related to the notion of *internal locus of control*—the sense one has of being in control of those things that influence his or her life.

People with a strong internal locus of control tend to believe they are in charge, that they control the out-comes in their life, and that their own skills, abilities, and efforts determine the bulk of their life experiences. They believe they can positively affect their beliefs, motivation, and performance in any area. In contrast, people with *external locus of control* believe that their lives are determined mainly by sources outside themselves—fate, chance, luck, or more powerful others.

Locus of control influences the way we view our opportunities and ourselves. People who feel they are in control are more upbeat, positive, outgoing, and opti-mistic. They see the opportunities in difficulties, rather than the difficulties in opportunities. When they wake up, they are more likely to say *"Goood Morrrnning God!"* than *"Good God, it's morning."*

These are the types of people I love to be around. Not only do they wake up in a more positive frame of mind, they demonstrate a number of other behaviours that are, in my experience, prerequisites for success.

They are strivers, willing to defer gratification and plan for the long term. Less prone to learned helplessness, they resist coercion, and are better at tolerating ambiguity. They tend to learn from past experiences, and are more willing to work on self-improvement and better themselves through remedial work. They are calculated risk takers who are more likely to be creative, innovative, and to initiate activity that makes things happen. After experiencing success, they tend to raise their behavioural goals. In addition, they work at developing and taking better advantage of support systems and networks—all in all, the kind of people you want to know and hang out with!

How do *you* get there? How do you develop an internal locus of control and cultivate these very positive characteristics? How do you walk through the door marked *freedom?*

You start by recognizing that your life is a product of the choices you've made—that you are, and have been, an active participant in the events of your life, not a victim of them. Second, accept that unless you're to the manor born, anything you want you're going to have to get through your own efforts. And third, understand there is a strong direct relationship between the material, emotional, and psychological rewards that accrue to you and the risks you take.

Now, don't get me wrong: I'm not recommending that you run off and quit your job, or something equally radical. In fact, you can probably accomplish everything you want to inside your present job. It will take some courage and behaviour change, but it can be done. I'm only suggesting that you examine all aspects of your life From any perspective—occupational, material, social, familial, spiritual—ask yourself:

- Am I doing what I want in my life?
- What is my level of commitment?
- Am I focusing my energies in the right areas?

If the answers are *no, under committed,* and *no,* then ask *why.* What's getting in the way? What are the constraints? What do you need to do differently? Which helmets do you need to remove to change the answers to *yes, highly committed,* and *yes?*

To be in control, you need to reframe some of what you believe and take your security helmet off! You need to take some risks—occupational, social, familial, religious, financial, physical—depending on what your expectations and aspirations are.

That darn security helmet! How to take it off?

You start by turning your dreams into goals. Make a written plan for their achievement that includes mileposts and, most importantly, deadlines. A dream without a deadline is still just a dream.

Inventory your resources. Determine what you have that will help you to get to where you want to go. Go get what you don't have.

Before you try something new, ask yourself the "horror floor" question: "If I tried this and failed, what's the worst that could happen?" Usually the worst that could happen isn't very bad at all, and, even if it is slightly terrifying, you can probably manage it.

Contrast the worst thing that could happen with the best possible outcome.

Learn to trust the process. Move in increments. Use small risks to create small wins and then bigger risks for bigger rewards. Success breeds success.

Start part-time. The advice I always give to people who want to go out on their own is "Have a good job." A good job will pay the bills until you develop your new venture to where it can sustain you and your family. If you are thinking of changing careers, look for opportunities to work in and learn more about the job you want. The same notions apply if you are interested in looking for different opportunities within your current employment situation.

Don't let your emotions rule your intellect. Do your due diligence. Calculate the risks. Count the alligators before you jump into the swamp, and make sure there aren't more than you can handle. A calculated risk is exactly what the words imply—you've calculated the risks associated with the move you're making and, to the best of your knowledge, the odds of success are in your favour.

Focus. Stay positive. Remember the Henry Fordism that "Whether you believe you can succeed or not, you are probably right." Use positive language. Visualize your success.

Get help. Look for seminars and courses that will help you. Find others who are trying to accomplish similar things, and share with them. Provide and accept wisdom and help. Turn your anxieties into energy and excitement. Use them to fuel the activity you need to succeed.

Celebrate your successes; learn from your setbacks and failures. At each milepost, review the processes you've used and the experiences you've had. Enhance what worked, and turn the setbacks into opportunities to learn.

And, as Nike used to say, just do it!

In a much-parodied scene from the movie *On the Waterfront,* in a conversation with his brother, Terry, a character played by a then much-more-buff Marlon Brando laments, with obvious sadness, "I coulda had class. I coulda been a contender. I coulda been somebody."

Woulda, coulda, shoulda—don't live your life wondering what could have been. Don't die with your helmet on. Be the somebody you are supposed to be!

> *Far better it is to dare mighty things, to win glorious triumphs, even though checkered by failure, than to take rank with those poor spirits who neither enjoy much nor suffer much because they live in the gray twilight that knows neither victory nor defeat.*
>
> —Theodore Roosevelt

A BIT OF AN END NOTE:

About the secret to successful marriage—there is a strong indirect relationship between the number of children a couple has and the likelihood of divorce. Couples that have no children have a sixty-percent divorce rate. Couples with one child have about a fifty-percent divorce rate. Couples with two children have about a forty-percent divorce rate. Couples with three children have about a ten-percent divorce rate, and couples with four children about a three-percent divorce rate. (From Mark Steyns mailbox.)

Chapter Two

Stella and Darwin, don't you dare leave this house without your helmet on

*If a man is alive, there is always danger that
he may die, though the danger must be allowed
to be less in proportion as he is dead-and-alive to
begin with. A man sits as many risks as he runs.*
—Henry David Thoreau

I like to read in the bathroom. It's quiet, reasonably comfortable, and the likelihood of being disturbed is almost zero. I mean, is anybody going to knock on the door and say, "I've got something I need to speak to you about—do you mind if I come in?" If patriotism is the last refuge of a scoundrel, then perhaps the bathroom is the last refuge for the pure privacy seeker.

An ideal privy design, in my view, would incorporate a few magazine racks, a writing desk, markers for high-lighting and underlining, and, if not a stock ticker, at least a television set tuned to an all-news channel.

I have my own bathroom—I inherited it from my kids when they left home. From a literary perspective, it's a microcosm of the public library. There is an eclectic collection of reading materials, ranging from a current newspaper or two through less-serious works such as *Dr. John's Bathroom Reader,* to heavier tomes like Alan Bloom's *Closing of the American Mind.* Something for everybody, you might say.

Included in the current collection, and one of my current favourites, is a copy of the *Darwin Awards,* given to me as a birthday present by my oldest daughter.

The Darwin Awards, as you probably know, are given posthumously to those who have the dubious dis-tinction of having done something that, while not only incredibly stupid, has taken them out of the gene pool— like the sound thinker who didn't put enough postage on a letter bomb and, when it came back marked "return to sender," opened the package. *Ka-Boom!* A one-way express ticket to his great reward. Did this guy need to get naked to count to twenty-one? I think so!

My favourite story—although the author of the piece only received an honorary Darwin because he did not die in the commission of his dim-witted act—is the one about the guy who tethered weather balloons to a lawn chair, strapped himself in and, armed with a six-pack of beer and a pellet gun, lifted off into the airspace over Los Angeles. (For these and other stories of amazing stupidity, check out www. darwinawards.com.)

It makes you wonder what kind of person gets up in the morning and says to his wife, "Hey, Maude, I've been wondering what to do with those weather balloons I bought on e-Bay—I think I'll tie them to the lawn chair and go flying." It's even scarier that his wife probably said, "Good idea, Stewart—wear a helmet." She was probably upset that they only owned one lawn chair. If stupidity hurt, these people would be in constant pain!

The hundreds, perhaps thousands, of stories recorded by the Darwin Awards people serve to support my contention that Darwin was wrong—we haven't evolved! Either that, or the award recipients are the missing links in the theory of human evolution.

Now, there are those who would say that we need to protect the Darwin Award winners and others of their ilk from themselves—that we should post "no diving!" signs at the shallow end of the gene pool. They would argue, for example, that had the instructions about handling the explosives been written more clearly, the letter-bomber would never have blown himself up, so it's not really his fault or responsibility. It's the manufacturers and they should pay. Or perhaps the letter bomber couldn't read well enough to follow instructions, and so the responsibility for his demise lies with the school system because it didn't teach him to read well. So, let's sue the system, the government, the language arts teachers, and anybody else we can think of!

To this way of thinking, regardless of what happens, the individual abdicates responsibility for any act. There is no internal locus of control. Rather than by individual choice, actions are predicated by outside forces—one's childhood, corporate irresponsibility, spouse, boss, whatever. It's the ultimate extension of 1970s comedian Flip Wilson's "the devil made me do it."

A quick visit to www.StellaAwards.com provides another example of the inability of people to assume responsibility for their own actions. Case in point: the fourth runner-up in the 2002 Stella Awards (named for Stella Liebeck, the woman who sued McDonalds because she was scalded by their coffee) was an obese, cigarette-smoking woman from Wilkes-Barre, PA, who has high blood pressure, high cholesterol, and a family history of coronary artery disease.

Although warned by doctors at the Department of Veterans Affairs Medical Centre of the seriousness of her condition, and counseled to eat less, exercise more, and stop smoking, she did little if anything to change her lifestyle. Surprise, surprise—she had a heart attack which, she says in a federal lawsuit, has left her a "cardiac invalid."

Unwilling to recognize her own culpability, she's suing eight doctors and their employer, the U.S. government, demanding a minimum of a million dollars in compensation. According to her, these medical care providers "did not do enough" to convince her to work to improve her own health.

Did not do enough? What more were the doctors in question supposed to do? And if they could have done more, who's to say this woman would have done anything positive in return?

Just as with the Darwin awards, there are thousands of candidates for the Stellas—each plumbing the depths of victimhood, saying, "I went out without my helmet on, and it's not my fault. The devil made me do it—now you have to fix it!" Do these people need helmets? Absolutely. Do we need helmets? Absolutely. Do those around us need helmets? Absolutely. But the responsibility for determining the size, design, and fit of the helmet should be that of each individual.

And what should we design these helmets to protect? We need to protect those things that are most important—our children, our futures, and ourselves.

Taking Care Of The Kids:

Children turn us into adults.

I had no idea what responsibility meant until our first daughter was born. Up to that point in my life, everything had been transitory or disposable. But the wrinkled, vernix-covered, incredibly beautiful little bundle my wife presented me with on that bright November day changed everything in a heartbeat.

For the first time ever, I met someone whom I instantly loved more than myself, and to whom I was inextricably linked for the rest of my life—someone to whom I would forever subordinate my needs. This was permanent! As my parents represented the past, my daughter represented the future. My wife and I were responsible for securing that future, and the kid didn't come with a manual!

Or a helmet!

It was going to be up to us to write the manual, and design and build the helmet. And we needed help! But where to go for help?

To the experts.

Now, when I say *experts*, I'm not talking about the usual suspects—academics, talk-show hosts, film stars, authors, "child care" professionals, and so on. Some of those people may have something to say, but heck, many of them don't even have children—or, if they do, the kids are often in the care of nannies!

I'm talking about those people in the trenches. Real people who, in the eyes of others, are doing a good, solid job of raising their children. They're parents of healthy, well-adjusted, successful children. They're people who give their children the helmets and the Kevlar vests needed to ward off the slings and arrows of the world, so they can safely grow into productive adults.

That's who we looked to—successful parents—and here's what they did.

They were leaders as well as parents. They didn't rely on the schools, the government, television, the movies, or music to teach their children values and the difference between right and wrong. They did it themselves.

They had a vision for their family and its future— one that they discussed and shared often, and supported with clearly articulated, clarified, and communicated values and beliefs. Every action, behaviour, and decision was taken with those values and beliefs firmly in mind. They constantly emphasized the relationship between family successes and acting in accordance with the values and beliefs. They made a clear distinction between right and wrong. Everybody was clear on how things were to be done, and why.

These parents were behavioural models for their children. Their behaviours reflected those that they wanted the kids to emulate. They were honest because they valued honesty; open because they valued open-ness; forgiving because they valued forgiveness. They made tough decisions when necessary, and they took responsibility for the results. They didn't just *tell* their children what to value and believe; they *showed* them through words and deeds.

They enabled their children. They communicated high-but-achievable behavioural and performance expectations, and provided the spiritual, emotional, physical, intellectual, and financial resources the children needed to successfully achieve them. They knew that self-esteem was a function of achievement.

They talked *with* their kids, not *at* them. They developed feedback loops, so the children could come to understand the impact of their behaviour on others. They made sure the kids understood the relationship between behaviour and consequences. And they distinguished between the child and his or her behaviour so that when there were problems, they would unconditionally love the child while looking for a solution to the problem.

They took pains to understand how children develop. As the children were finding their way in the world, these parents assessed their children's maturity and skill levels and provided firm direction when needed; discussed when the circumstances merited; pushed the kids away and let them make provisional tries when they were ready to, and finally, set them free altogether. Through it all, the door was left open for the kids to come back if they needed to.

They took an active role in their children's education, both formal and informal. They were active contributors to both the schools and communities. They enriched the home environment in every way they could. They went to concerts, games, on camping trips, and, unfailingly, to the ceremonies that marked the graduations from one stage to the next.

Finally, although their children were outstanding in any number of ways, these parents freely admitted the kids were anything but perfect. They accepted and openly talked about the fact that, while good kids, their children were just as prone as others to the vicissitudes of growing up and, on occasion, their behaviour would reflect that fact.

And when the time came, they discussed the future and provided appropriate advice and guidance regarding career and other life-choices that children must eventually make. Through it all, they encouraged independent, critical thinking so, in the final analysis, each child became his or her own person.

And there was no extended adolescence—the kids were gone by their early-to mid-twenties, coming back only to visit, usually with families of their own. Unlike the "kidults" and "adultescents" so prevalent today, they became mature adults ready to take on responsibility and commit to careers and relationships.

It was to these parents that we looked to for guidance, to provide us with a manual. And, did it work? Unequivocally, *yes!*

Are our children perfect? Unequivocally, *no!* But they turned out pretty darn good. Although different as chalk and cheese, both are bright, ambitious, happy young women who are diligently working toward their respective life-goals. Each is principled, charitable, and empathic. They can read, write, and think! We're immensely proud of both.

Any difficulties or rough spots along the way? Absolutely! Did we have problems dealing with the stresses of parenting? Some, but nothing debilitating. Whatever we had, we were able to manage; and, in the end, my wife and I are comfortable in the knowledge that we provided our children with what they needed to ensure a safe, happy, comfortable childhood, and to jump-start a productive adulthood.

Taking Care Of Ourselves:

But what about ourselves?

Protecting ourselves is equally as important as protecting our children. If adults cannot function well, they are of little use to children. And what limits our functioning? Stress—that insidious, energy-sapping, career-limiting, relationship-destroying phenomenon that seems to afflict almost everybody.

Most people will admit an inverse relationship between their levels of happiness and stress, effectiveness and stress, and productivity and stress. The more of one you have, the less of the other. The answer to the question, "What do you need to be better?" is usually "less stress."

So, we need a "stress helmet."

I should be stressed!! At least that's what people tell me. I travel constantly, eat too many restaurant meals, sleep in too many different beds in too many different hotels, and constantly deal with the jet lag that comes from crossing back and forth across different time zones. On top of all that, I've chosen a line of work characterized by uncertainty!

All of my money is tied up in small, high-risk companies. I once watched my net worth plunge a half million dollars in less than a month. I have considerable (but not insurmountable) debt. I'm somewhat of a libertarian living in a nanny state.

And this morning, I can't open the trunk of my car because the strap from my grandson's hockey bag is caught in the lock. (Trivial, to be sure, but have you ever noticed how the little things can really set you off?)

But—hold the stress tabs! I don't need them. I'm not at all stressed. In fact, I'm probably the least stressed person you're likely to meet. I'm very comfortable with myself, sleep well at night, even when the stock market is in turmoil, and, for a person my age, am in reasonably good physical shape. The only thing that might be mistaken for stress is my odd foray into curmudgeonly behaviour. I'm not really a curmudgeon—it's just that, at a certain age, you can be just about anything you want. People will write it off as some sort of premature dementia.

And I'm not on cheap drugs or prescription medication!

Why am I not stressed out? Because I subscribe to the Hans Selye notion that stress is a response rather than a condition. So stress is not like the flu—rather, it is the manifestation of one's response to having the flu. And I can choose how I respond to being sick. I can see it as an insurmountable, somewhat permanent difficulty, or a temporary condition that, with proper rest and treatment, I will soon overcome. In the latter situation I control the flu, in the former it controls me.

The more I feel in control, the less the situation negatively affects me. A healthy, productive response to a negative situation or circumstance, then, is to shift from a sense of being acted upon by external forces that are out of your control, to one of acting from an internal conviction or energy that enables you to take charge. Even better, if I take proactive steps to control the likelihood of getting the flu, I won't have to worry about the response, because none will be necessary. So, to the extent I can, my best strategy is to control the conditions that have the potential to negatively affect me. Simply knowing that is the first step in designing and building the "stress helmet."

What one needs, then, is, in a figurative sense, to avoid getting the flu—in other words, effectively manage those situations that you let get out of control. And the best way to do that is to do a better job of managing priorities and, in the parlance of Stephen Covey, "put first things first."

To do this one needs to understand something that I first learned from my wife, and later had confirmed by Covey: the interaction between *urgency*—the window of time that is available to get things done—and *importance*—the impact of what needs to be done on ourselves, our family, our work, and so on.

More often than not, I think, we make ourselves subject to the tyranny of the urgent, and as a result, we spend too much of our time operating in crisis mode. And the outcome of crisis is often, if not usually, feelings of stress.

What's needed is a way to minimize either the sense or reality of constantly being hurried. How to do that? By concentrating on what's really important.

A financial example may best illustrate the point. Is saving for retirement important? Clearly, the answer is yes! When should one start saving for retirement—earlier or later? "That's a no-brainer," you say. "Earlier, of course." Why? Because of the magic of compounding. If you put a little money away each year, starting in your twenties, you'll have much more at your chosen retirement age than if you wait until your forties to start saving.

There's no urgency when you're twenty—retirement is a long way off. But at forty-five or fifty, it's just around the corner and, if you haven't prepared, saving the money you're going to need to retire becomes not only important, but also incredibly urgent! The impact is great; the temporal window is closing and the anxiety, a.k.a. stress level, rises.

Taking care of the important things before they become urgent is like getting a flu shot. You're being proactive; anticipating the future and taking steps to control it. What are these important things? Anniversaries, children's birthdays, performance reviews, regular meetings with your staff (if you have staff), children's concerts and sporting events, calls to your parents and other family members, time for personal reflection and spiritual rejuvenation, vacations and so on—these are things that need to be scheduled and the time to do them considered sacrosanct. Ensuring you do the important but less-urgent things first gives you the flexibility and ability to more comfortably and capably cope when crisis situations pop up—although by doing this you'll have fewer of those than you might think.

A few examples from my own experience might be instructive. When my children were growing up, I never missed a birthday, concert, or parent-teacher interview. I diarized those events at the beginning of the year, and took steps to ensure that I would always be available for them. By doing it early and making those times unavailable for other activities, I avoided any conflict—and we know what conflict leads to!

I schedule performance management sessions with my staff (when it's necessary for me to have a staff) at the beginning of new projects, to ensure that my expectations and those of the client are clear. I hold informal project update sessions daily, and formal meetings once a week. I conduct formal performance reviews at specified times.

I hold these meetings because they are *important*—not because they are *urgent*. For all involved, conducting our work lives in this way helps us to anticipate problems before they occur and, as a result, we can take action that eliminates them or minimizes their effect.

When my parents were alive, I called them every Sunday at 11:00 a.m. sharp, regardless of where I was in the world. Why? Because they were the only parents I had, and it was important both that I talked to them and they heard from me. Like many parents, as they got older, they lived somewhat vicariously through my siblings and me. I think they got a charge out of receiving calls from England, France, or whatever other part of the world I was in when I phoned.

After my mother passed on, I continued to telephone my father at the same time every Sunday. Most often we had nothing new to say to each other, but we both enjoyed the experience. I was in Texas the last time I called him. When he answered the phone, my father told me he couldn't move his legs. I contacted my brother, who took Dad to the hospital. There, we discovered that he had suffered a series of strokes. He died four weeks later.

Because I talked to my parents every week, I had no sense we had left anything unsaid when each passed away. There was no urgency at the end; no trying to make up for lost time. Those many very *important*, but never *urgent*, Sunday calls made sure of that.

Within each of the roles we play—father, mother, wife, husband, friend, son, daughter, sibling, friend, coworker, employee, employer—there is an array of things and events that are *important*, but not *urgent*. Identifying these and making sure they are taken care of first is a surefire way to control the circumstances that contribute to the sense of disease so often associated with stress. In simple terms, it is priority management: manage your priorities; reduce your sense of stress.

The Future:

"You can be poor when you're young, but you can't be poor when you're old." That was the tag line used some years ago in a financial services television commercial. Truer words were never spoken. I was relatively poor when I was young. Just about everybody I knew was, and it was kind of fun. We lived an almost communal lifestyle, sharing money, accommodation, food, beer, cigarettes, and other essentials of post-pubescent life. Would I think it was as much fun if I had to do it all again today? *Could* I do it all again? Not on your life!

When you're young, it's easy to live in the moment, but as you grow older, unless you're one of the afore-mentioned "kidults" or "adultescents," life becomes more complex. The time comes to respond to Paul of Tarsus' admonition to "put away childish things," become an adult, and assume adult responsibilities. Among those is the responsibility to protect the future for you and your family—to design and build a financial security helmet.

Now, I'm anything but a financial genius. However, there are five basic principles that we learned and used to design and build a "financial future" helmet. And while we're far from wealthy, I have every confidence that we will not have to live in a refrigerator box whenever I quit working, and that my wife will be able to comfortably carry on in the event of my premature demise. (You should know: I'm at an age where I think eighty-five is a premature death!)

Is designing and building such a helmet akin to rocket surgery? Absolutely not—you need to do five key things to get started:

First, determine your short-and long-term financial goals. Start by taking a comprehensive snapshot of your current situation—your assets, net income, debts, and living expenses. Once you've done this, you can start setting long-

and short-term financial goals. Decide what lifestyle you want to enjoy between now and when you retire; what retirement lifestyle you expect to have, and what sort of education you expect to provide for your children.

Second, after you've assessed where you are now and where you want to be in the future, take steps to protect your ability to get there, and stay there once you've arrived—a major part of your family's financial program to insure against major financial loss.

Now, I will admit that I haven't always been a big fan of insurance—I've often referred to it as a wager where you bet that something's going to happen and the insurance company bets that it won't. But exposure to available research on the numbers of people who become disabled, need home care, or suffer from cancer, heart, or respiratory disease, along with stories from any number of grieving spouses, has made me acutely aware of the fact there are simply no guarantees against serious illness, accidents, or untimely death. So, take the necessary steps to insure against loss of life, loss of income, and loss of physical assets.

Third, pay yourself first. This is something that my father did religiously throughout his working life and, as a result, for a guy who never earned more than five dollars an hour, he piled up an exceptional asset base. "It's not what you earn—it's what you keep," was his mantra. His suggestion was to save at least ten percent of pre-tax income—more if possible. His counsel to me was to pay down my mortgage as quickly as possible, especially in times of low interest. And he was right. In the short term, you'll be better off reducing a mortgage that costs you six percent than earning around a taxable 1.5 percent (or less) in a savings account.

Maximize your RSP, IRA or 401K contributions every year, and make the contribution at the beginning rather than at the end of the year. Simply doing that will substantially increase the size of your retirement nest egg when you're ready to cash out.

Fourth, avoid credit traps. If you use credit cards, always pay any money owing before interest is due. Consider paying off your credit card immediately if you have money in a savings account—as with the mortgage, the interest earned on the savings is certain to be lower than what's charged by the credit card company. Avoid using credit cards for cash advances. Usually the interest charges are higher for these, and the charges begin immediately. If you do carry a balance on your cards, try to negotiate a lower rate with the credit card company. If you need money urgently, it's usually cheaper to negotiate a personal loan with your bank or credit union.

Finally, protect your family in the event of your death. Make a Will. If you die without leaving a Will, in all likelihood, the only thing you'll really leave your loved ones is a bloody mess—one that could take many years and a whole bunch of money to sort out.

Without a Will, the courts and government will decide how your property and possessions will be divided. I would expect there are two chances of them acting in a way consistent with what your wishes might have been: slim and none!

Making a Will doesn't mean the Grim Reaper is about to pay you a visit. It simply means that your affairs will be sorted out in the ways you want, and as a result, you can go about your life with a peaceful mind because your loved ones are protected.

These five principles are only a starting point—a few suggestions that any financial management professional can improve and expand upon. If I have one regret about how we've handled our financial affairs over time, it is not enlisting enough professional help. When we were starting, the financial management business was neither as big nor as sophisticated as it is today. Who knows, with better help, I might be writing this from some warm Caribbean tax haven rather than in a cold Calgary office! "Don't try this alone— use a trained professional" absolutely is the best advice I'm really qualified to give.

So, there you go—helmets for what you really need to protect: your family, yourself, and your future. Don't leave home without them.

> *There are only two lasting bequests*
> *we can hope to give our children.*
> *One is roots; the other, wings.*
> —Hodding Carter

Chapter Three

Doris

The farther back you look,
the further ahead you can see.
—Winston Churchill

Shortly after the end of the First World War, my mother, two older siblings, her father, pregnant mother, and two younger children ("the babies," as they were called) sailed out of Bristol Harbour bound for a new life in Canada. Almost immediately after arriving in Halifax, they boarded a train and made the long journey to Western Canada, where my grandfather found work as a miner in Pocahontas, a little town near Jasper. My grandmother gave birth to a sixth child, a little girl; the family, now eight strong, began to settle into their new life in Canada.

Everybody in the household had a job. The two oldest cleaned, helped with washing and cooking, chopped wood, and hauled water. My mother's job was to watch the babies: change diapers, keep them out of trouble, and get them to sleep at naptime. While two of the babies dropped off without any trouble, little Kathleen needed to stroke my mother's face and tug on her ear before she could sleep.

Although a somewhat of a struggle, life was fairly routine and uneventful—until the morning my grandfather failed to show up for breakfast. In his place at the kitchen table was a note telling my grandmother to pack up the children and join him at the Alberta Hotel in Edmonton.

Now, Edmonton wasn't Bristol, but in my grandmother's mind, it beat the hell out of Pocahontas. Pleased with the prospect of leaving small-town life and excited by whatever opportunity her husband had found in the city, she hurriedly packed up her brood and traveled eastward.

She was surprised, but not alarmed, that her husband wasn't there to meet them, or even registered, when they arrived at the Alberta Hotel in Edmonton. She was confident that he was on his way, and that their wait would be a short one.

She never saw him again. It was twenty-five years before *anyone* saw my grandfather again.

Six children, no husband, no immediate family to fall back on, no money, and no prospects! A woman in similar circumstances today would quickly place a call to social services, and in short order a myriad of services and resources would be available to her. That would work today, but not 1920.

Tongues wagged; questions were asked. How were they living? Were the children being fed? Were they being brought up properly? Without a husband, was it even *possible* that children could be brought up properly? "Probably not," agreed the powers that be. They needed to do something.

And they did. What passed for social services at that time deemed that a woman in such circumstances could not possibly provide those things necessary to good parenting. On a sunny summer Saturday afternoon, my mother and my aunts and uncles were taken away from my grandmother, and placed in government care. My grandmother never saw the babies again.

While the six children, separated from each other for the first time in their young lives, tried to make sense of what had happened, my grandmother, helpless to stop what was happening, kept a vigil outside the "orphanage." And wept.

In the end, the babies—Kathleen, Pearl and Clarence —were put up for adoption, and my mother and her older siblings were separated and placed in foster homes—foster farms, actually. They moved my mother to a farm in central Alberta, where she learned to cook for farm crews during harvest. One of the children, but never one of the family, she worked the farm during the day. At night, in her bed, she read *Anne of Green Gables* and dreamed of what it would be like to be Anne Shirley, the heroine of Lucy Maud Montgomery's fabulous stories.

It was 1920. My mother was eight years old. Anne Shirley was her rock. It would be sixty-four years before she saw the babies again.

My mom, her older brother, and her sister were released from foster care when they each turned sixteen. Within a few years, they had reconnected with one another and with their mother, but soon they were leading separate lives. People grew up more quickly in those days. My mother went to work, met and married my father, and by age nineteen had begun to have babies of her own. Of her six children, five survived: one girl and four boys.

Raising her children became my mother's focus. Always supportive, she held us closely, both physically and emotionally, never giving up on any of us, always giving us another chance. She was the same with the grandchildren that came along as my older brothers and sister grew into adulthood.

Although she loved all of her grandchildren, the first-born—my oldest brother's daughter—was her favourite. When his marriage failed and my brother's ex-wife moved to Vancouver, taking their daughter with her, we were all upset —but my mother's hurt was palpable. For her, it was déjà vu.

We didn't know—none of us, not even my father, knew— anything of her story. My mother and her older siblings kept everything in present tense. They didn't talk about the past. It was their secret, one kept close because of the shame and indignity they felt about having been wards of the state.

My uncle died first and, about ten years later, my aunt passed on. My mother, having no one left to talk to about the babies, was left alone to wonder what had happened to them.

What had happened to the babies? Kathleen, the little girl who needed to stroke my mother's face and tug on her ear before falling asleep, was taken to the West Coast where she was brought up as Fran. An English remittance man and his wife adopted Pearl. They changed her name to Virginia, and she went with them when they returned to England. Clarence also ended up on the West Coast, where his adoptive parents tried without success to change his name to Michael. It seems Clarence was Clarence, and no amount of reward, threat, or cajoling was going to get him to respond to any other name.

Although never told that she was adopted, Kathleen always felt a little different from the rest of her family. The feeling nagged at her long into her adult years, and finally she confronted her adoptive parents. She learned the truth, and, as they say, "the truth shall set you free." Kathleen went on a mission— her goal, to find her birth family.

Not an easy task, at a time when governments kept adoption records sealed, and the experts and bureaucrats of the day strongly discouraged efforts to find one's birth family. It was more difficult and frustrating than tilting at windmills, but Kathleen was nothing if not persistent. She wrote letters, made phone calls, got in the faces of the social workers and bureaucrats, wrote more letters, and made more phone calls. Finally, in the early 1980s, the Alberta government broke the seal on the adoption files and allowed many people, including Kathleen, a brief peek at the past. But it was just a peek.

She found out that she did, indeed, have brothers and sisters, but she could not contact them directly. Contact could only be initiated or agreed to by one of them. Unfortunately, social services didn't know where any of them were, or even if they were alive or dead.

Serendipity, synchronicity, God's hand—call it what you like: just as Kathleen was about to give up, Alberta's Vital Statistics received a request from an English woman named Virginia Vaughn. She was applying for her British pension, and needed her birth certificate to provide proof of age. Knowing that she was born in Canada, but not aware that her English parents had adopted her, Virginia was about to find out about the past—that in fact, she had been adopted!

Her first reaction was one of disbelief. She had planned a trip to Seattle, and offered to stop in Edmonton on the way to prove the government wrong and claim her birth certificate. The stop was brief and the government's information convincing. They told Virginia about her sister Kathleen's inquiries and asked if she'd like to meet her. The answer, of course, was "yes."

A few days later, in Vancouver, the two sisters had lunch together—for the first time in sixty-four years. Encouraged by this success, Kathleen's rallying cry became "Find the rest of them!" She suggested searching pension records, and there they found my mother's name. My mom received two telephone calls on the same day—one from Vancouver, and one from England. She finally was able to talk to her sisters, after sixty-four years.

Kathleen visited my mother. It was amazing: two people, separated by so many years, each with the same speech patterns, the same way of sitting, the same way of holding a cigarette and making gestures. They spent two days trying to make up sixty-four years. On the third day, they went to thank social services for bringing them together. There was a surprise waiting for them when they arrived: "We've found Clarence, and he wants to talk to you."

They made the call, and the two sisters talked to their brother for the first time in sixty-four years.

It was wonderful, exhilarating, and special—but, at the same time, bittersweet. Separated as children, they had been reunited as old people. They had been a family, but now they were strangers. How do you make up for all that lost time? How do you tell all the stories? You have a giant reunion, and we planned one. On the West Coast, over the New Year. The extended families of the four survivors all came.

The spotlight was on my mother. She knew the story; she had pictures of their parents. The story was told and retold, the pictures shown again and again. The secret was out, and people jumped on the details like wolves on a lamb chop! I think my mother talked non-stop for four days.

We had a great party. Uncle Clarence played his squeezebox; we sang, danced, ate, and did all the other stuff that families do when they get together. It was a special time for all of us, but especially for my mother and the babies— under one roof again… after sixty-four years.

When my daughter graduated from Yale, a speaker reminded her class that they were now part of a group that extended back to 1703—one through which the threads of Yale rites, rituals, traditions, values, and stories are woven. "Do not break the threads," she told them. "As Yale graduates, you are expected to move into the future with proper respect for the past. Knowing where you've come from helps you to know better who you are, and makes it easier to get to where you're going," seemed to be the message.

It's not any different for the rest of us. We need to know where we've come from. Almost every family has a history of hardship, perseverance, devotion, and of adherence to principles, values, and faith. We need to know this to understand where we fit in time, why we believe what we believe, why we value what we value, and where some of our more idiosyncratic behaviours came from.

The same is true for organizations. You should know the history of your company—why and how it was started, the hardships it suffered, and the successes it realized. Learn about the heroes and goats; learn and perpetuate the corporate myths.

This history instructs our lives. If we know where we came from, we know more about why we are the way we are-and it will be easier to get to where we're going. We need to know our history.

Just as Kathleen needed to know the stories and see the pictures, so do we, if we are to understand our place in the lifeline. Our parents link us with the past, and our children link us to the future.

We need to recognize, celebrate, create, preserve, and pass on family histories. We need to tell the family stories—the stories that provide examples of our family's philosophies and value systems; stories that give us a sense of belonging and teach us to accept ourselves as we are. Stories that honour individual lives, experiences, and relationships; that celebrate the accomplishments and pass along lessons learned from the struggles. Stories that connect us to our history, give us a sense of where we've come from and how we fit in, and explain our family character.

My wife has recorded our lives together, both in words and in pictures. She keeps a daily diary—little tidbits that help us remember what happened on a particular date last year or the year before. We have threescore and more albums filled with photos of our parents and grandparents, siblings, kids, friends, and family. They're found on coffee tables, couches, chairs, on top of stereo speakers, and in bookshelves. They're better than television. Much better.

At any given time, someone will open one up to reflect on what was, ask questions about the people and events captured in the photos, and tell or listen to the stories associated with the pictures. Our personal histories come alive.

Before my grandson met his maternal great-grand parents, he knew about them from the pictures we showed him and the stories we told him. He knew them in history before he got to know them in person. Knowing where he's come from will help him understand who he is, and will make it easier to get to where he's going.

Keep and celebrate your history.

> *Now go, write it before them in a table and note it in a book, that it may be for the time to come forever and ever.*
> —Isaiah 30:8

AS A BIT OF AN EPILOGUE:

- Kathleen is the only one of the babies still alive.

- My grandfather—that's another story—maybe even a book!

- Five days after telling the stories at the reunion, my mother had a major stroke. She never spoke again.

- My sister's name is Shirley Anne.

- My grandson likes to stroke my cheek and tug on my ear before he goes to sleep.

Tom Olson

Chapter Four

the eagle, the duck, and the dream merchant

*Twenty years from now you will be more
disappointed by the things that you didn't do
than by the ones you did do. So throw off
the bowlines. Sail away from the safe harbour.
Catch the trade winds in your sails.
Explore. Dream. Discover.*

—Mark Twain

I like flying.

I like everything about airplanes—taking off, landing, the noises, the smells, the seating arrangements, the tiny little bags of nuts, the bad coffee, even the mostly inedible food. It's a good thing too, because I spend a lot of time in jetliners.

One of the things I've noticed is the passenger cabin of an aircraft is usually a very quiet place. People work, read, stare glassy-eyed at the seatback in front of them. They do just about anything except talk to their seatmates—until flight attendants deliver the food. As people begin to peel back the foil wrap on the little trays of mystery meat, conversations start—conversations that usually centre on questions such as, "What do you think this is? No, really?" and, "Do you think that this chicken died of natural causes?" or, "Mine looks like it's already been eaten!"

The noise level rises, and sometime after the remains of the meal have been removed, the talk continues—usually nothing too serious, threatening, deep, or meaningful, just a surface level exploration of each other's lives. Often, because it's unlikely that you'll ever see each other again, the conversations are quite candid.

What do people talk about, mostly? Work! And, according to the official airline guide to pleasant but non-threatening conversation, the first question you ask is "What do you do?" Because I don't like to break protocol, that's the very question I prepared to ask my seatmate on a recent trip home (after we cleared up the initial confusion about what *exactly* we were eating, of course).

She was a woman in her mid to late thirties, I would guess. From her confident demeanor, well-tailored, conservative suit, and large three-ring binder under her arm, I guessed that she was a bank employee on her way home from some corporate training event. Except we were in the business-class cabin—a place where you don't often find bank employees. Before I could ask, however, she turned in her seat, extended her hand, and said, "Hi! My name's Sheila, and I am a Dream Merchant."

Now, I have been beaten to the punch on "What do you do?" once or twice; I had even had the odd high-disclosure types tell what they did before I could ask. But this was the first time I'd met a Dream Merchant!

"A dream merchant?" I asked—"What does a Dream Merchant do, and how come she's flying business class?"

She smiled and said, "Simple—I help make people's dreams come true. And being in business class is a reward for doing just that."

Helps make people's dreams come true, I thought. "What an interesting idea. Does it pay well?" I asked.

"Not as much as I would like, but the work is rewarding, the working conditions are excellent, and my clients are very happy—and I have lots of repeat and referral business."

"It must require a great deal of training," I ventured, looking around for any sign of a magic wand or pouch of pixie dust.

"Oh, yes," she said, "some is self-taught, but for the most part, my company takes care of it."

A company! She was a Dream Merchant for a Dream Merchant company! I didn't even know there were companies selling dreams! *I could work for a company like that,* I thought—*a dream company; nice loosey-goosey environment, lots of happy interesting, creative people mixing up potions and inventing incantations that would help the masses fulfill their unrequited desires.*

What a company! What a job!

"I have a dream," I said excitedly, sounding more than a little like Martin Luther King. "Could you hook me up with Jennifer Aniston?"

"Jennifer Aniston! Men…! If I could, I would," she said with a twinkle, "but I don't have that kind of stroke. However, if it helps, I can hook you up with your dream house, dream car, dream vacation, help you send your kids to their dream college, or get you closer to the retirement you've always dreamed of."

Now in truth, at my age, getting hooked up with Jennifer Aniston would scare the life out of me. I already live in a great house, and have another in the mountains, drive a two-seater, and every holiday I take turns out to be a dream vacation. But the retirement I'd always dreamed of...

"*That's* something I'd like to talk about!" I told her.

She looked pleased and excited at the same time. "I'd love to talk about it with you—why don't you call me later this week?" And she handed me her card.

I took the card. *Nothing special,* I thought. It was just a little white rectangle —blank—nothing on it. I stared at it, thinking there must be some trick—some invisible chemical that would react to the oils in my fingers and, as if by magic, bring up the name and logo of the dream-merchant company and the contact information for my magic-making seatmate.

Nothing happened. I stared harder, and vigorously rubbed my thumb across the entire surface of the card. Still nothing.

"You're looking at the wrong side of the card," she said. "Turn it over."

"Oh," I offered sheepishly. "I thought that... oh, never mind." Slowly I turned the card over, still expecting something magical, interesting, and creative.

And there it was. At the top of the card was her employer's name and logo. I looked at it, momentarily stunned into silence. She worked for a bank!

A bank!

"Y-you w-work for a bank," I stammered. "You told me you were a Dream Merchant! It doesn't say 'Dream Merchant' on your card—it says, 'Personal Financial Services Officer.' When I asked you what you did, why didn't you just say you were a personal financial services officer for a bank?"

"Personal Financial Services Officer—oh, that's my job title," she said, "but that's not really what I do. What I really do is help people find the money they need to buy their houses, cars, good educations for their children, and so on. These are all the stuff of dreams. And I do it by arranging loans, helping with investments, connecting them with financial advisors, and arranging terms and conditions that are most suitable for them. And when I'm finished, people get what they want, what they dreamed of. They're happy."

She explained more about her job, and how banking had changed in the years since she'd started. It had gone from a business that was mostly transactional to one that was competitive, sales-driven, and customer focused. Starting as a teller, she had worked her way through positions of increasing responsibility until she was promoted to her current job.

While she was happy with the promotion, she was really concerned about how she would handle those parts of the job that required her to make cold calls and attend receptions, investment seminars, and other functions where she would be expected to put on her "bank face," work the crowd, and attempt to solicit new business.

"I'd never been asked to do anything like that before," she told me. "And, at first, I was anything but successful. Introducing myself as a Personal Financial Services Officer in a room full of Personal Financial Officers wasn't very helpful—often, people just stifled a yawn and quickly changed the conversation, or simply found some polite reason to move away. It seemed nobody wanted to hear about what either the bank or I had to offer. This failure was a new experience for me, and I was not taking it lightly. The harder I tried, the more frustrated I became. I was ready to quit."

"But you didn't."

"No... I decided to take a vacation. I've always found that if I take a little time off and separate myself from the problem for a while, I gain some perspective and can think more clearly. So, I rented a little place on a beautiful mountain lake, where I could sit with my morning coffee, watch the mist rise off the lake, and think things over.

"One morning, as I sat pondering my future, inside the dock area I saw a group of eighteen or so Merganser ducklings; you know, the ones with the little hoods or tufts on their heads. Mergansers, I've been told, are communal. They share responsibilities in their flocks. One adult duck had apparently been given the babysitting assignment for that morning, and was obviously teaching them to do 'duck things.'

"It was really cute, and fun to watch. They would all swim together in a line; when the adult bobbed for food, the whole group would bob. If the mother duck made a left turn, they all made a left turn. When it was time to go up on shore, they would all go up together. Suddenly, in the midst of this little show, out of the corner of my eye I saw a bald eagle in full dive. There was a small splash as he hit the water—it seemed to me more of a ripple, actually—and in less than a second, the eagle rose from the water's surface with a huge fish clenched firmly in his talons. It cut a little circle in the morning sky, and then flew away to places unknown to have his breakfast, or do whatever eagles do with the fish they catch. It was really incredible!

"How different were these birds! The Mergansers with their communal behaviour, the seemingly carefully orchestrated, coordinated little routines were such a contrast with the eagle's behaviour. He was on his own. It seemed to me that he just circled in the sky, waiting to see what he wanted to see in the lake, and then, "BAM!" he just dove down and took it! No discussion with the other eagles, no asking for permission, as it were. Then it hit me: I needed to be an eagle!

"But what I was—was a duck! An eager duck, but a duck nonetheless. Everything I did was indistinguishable from all the other ducks. We all looked the same, dressed pretty much the same, introduced ourselves in the same way, sold the same products and services using the same sales techniques, regardless of which bank we worked for. In a sense, you could say we all bobbed for food the same way. I suppose, if you listened carefully to the noise at some of the receptions we all attended, what you'd really hear was a cacophony of quacking!

"To be successful, I knew I needed to be as different from the ducks as the eagle was... and is. I needed to position myself differently—in a way that made me stand out. I also needed to position the bank differently, show how we offered things none of our competitors did. I needed to be different—in short, to position myself in a way that differentiated me from all the other Personal Financial Officers.

"In other words," she went on, "I realized that I couldn't position myself as an invaluable resource by using title or products and services. Positioning myself in that way has no differentiating value—it only puts me in the same arena with all other financial service providers—puts me in the company of ducks.

"I decided that I needed to make it clear what clients could expect from a relationship with me—the application of a unique combination of skills and resources that enable me to quickly and effectively deliver the outcomes or benefits that they are looking for."

"So you became a Dream Merchant," I responded.

"Well, not right away. It took me a while to think through the process. I talked to a lot of people, did some reading, looked at what other successful people did, and found a mentor. In the final analysis, I decided that I would be more successful if, among other things, I started defining myself in terms of the outcomes I created rather than the things I did.

"At first, if people asked me what I did, I'd simply tell them 'I help people get what they want to get out of life,' and let the conversation move on from there. It worked—I mean, who doesn't want that? The Dream Merchant tag came from a client after I'd arranged a new home mortgage for her and her husband. Being able to finally build this new home was a dream come true for them, and I, in her words, was the 'Dream Merchant who made it possible.' It became my *'brand,'* and I've used it since then. Got *you* interested, didn't it?"

"It certainly did," I admitted, "but wasn't that kind of risky? 'I'm a Dream Merchant' or 'I make people happy' is hardly the kind of thing one expects a banker to say."

"Oh, I was a little uncomfortable at first, but you know what they say: no risk, no reward. And the benefits of differentiating and branding myself like this far outweigh whatever risk I take. Plus, it's fun."

"And all of this has worked for you? I mean, it's made it easier for you to sell the bank's products and services?"

"Absolutely," she said. "But you know, I really don't *sell* anything."

"You don't?" I stammered. "At the end of the day, isn't that what you're really supposed to do—sell the bank's products and services?"

"Of course," she replied, "but really, nobody wants to be sold anything, do they? I simply create the opportunity for people to buy."

Now, I had never heard someone in a sales job say this before. I always thought that salespeople sold stuff—products, services, and so on.

She went on to explain that, to her way of thinking, the satisfaction people have with a product or service is directly related to the extent to which they feel the decision to buy it was theirs. Selling, in her view, was doing something *to* people. Creating the opportunity to buy was doing something *with* them—a process characterized by collaboration or partnership. To her, creating the opportunity to buy involved a gaining a deeper understanding of what clients really needed, and then demonstrating how she and her bank, in combination, were better positioned to satisfy these needs than anyone else. She always left the decision with the customer, never tried to talk anybody into anything.

In her words, "Someone's need to buy is more important than my need to sell. People need to feel they are in control, and I let them control the decision-making process. It's easier for them to live with their own decisions than to try to live with ones I make for them."

There was a familiar bump as the wheels touched the ground, and we began to taxi to the terminal. I was sorry the conversation was ending. I realized that I had been in the company of a very bright and astute woman who had taught me some very important things. The conversation ended too soon, but that's the nature of airplane talk.

Now, all of this was brought to mind because of the following lament that I heard from two very bright, capable, but different people within the space of one week. One is a middle-aged woman living in North America. The other is a man in his late twenties living in the United Kingdom.

To paraphrase: "I used to believe that if I were conscientious, worked hard, achieved my goals, and was a good example to others in the organization, I would succeed in this company. I've been and done all of those things, and I'm languishing—others less qualified are passing me by. I'm frustrated. I need to do a better job of selling myself, but I don't know how!"

Please understand that these people are qualified. Each graduated from highly regarded universities; my North American friend attended Queen's, and the young man from the United Kingdom went to Cambridge. Both have master's degrees. Not too shabby!

Both are personable, highly articulate, widely read and well mannered. They are experienced in their respective fields.

Each knows which fork to use and the difference between a Claret glass and a Sherry glass.

Neither have any slovenly or disgusting personal habits. They bathe regularly and dress well.

They have all the professional and personal qualities needed to rocket them through just about any organization, but they can't seem to get off the launch pad.

How to get off the launch pad—a few things my dream merchant seatmate did may help. First, she developed a *Personal Value Proposition.* What is a Personal Value Proposition? According to Sheila, it's a description of how one's unique mixture of five key elements creates and/or adds value for an organization and the people in it.

For you, these elements include:

1. The knowledge you have about the events and trends in areas critical to or of most interest to your company and clients.
2. The kinds of internal and external networks that you can tap into to meet corporate/client needs.
3. Your ability to generate and implement superior solutions to organizational issues and concerns;
4. The academic, technical, or interpersonal tools you can bring to bear in key situations; and finally,
5. The personal attributes and strengths you have that set you apart from others in the organization.

A personal examination of these elements affirms and provides direction at the same time. It *affirms* because it reminds you of all the strong, positive things you bring to the table. It *provides direction* because it points out the gaps you need to close before you can position yourself more effectively.

Sheila realized she needed to do this kind of personal stocktaking when she decided to differentiate herself. With the help of her boss, colleagues, husband, and others, she examined each element separately, combined all the data, and created a succinct summary of what she had to offer. She took steps to both improve her strengths and erase the gaps she'd identified. After all of that, she could confidently express the advantages she brought—what made her a valuable resource. She had begun the process of creating a personal brand!

She fashioned a one-line proclamation, a marketing slogan if you like, that reflected the outcomes she would create for her clients. She incorporated her slogan, *"Helping people get what they want to get out of life—one client at a time,"* into all of her correspondence, electronic and otherwise. When asked what she did, instead of replying that she was a Personal Financial Services Officer, she would answer, *"I help people get what they want to get out of life—one client at a time."* After her client's comments about making dreams come true, she prefaced her introduction with the Dream Merchant phrase—and now, she simply says, "Dream Merchant."

Articulating her personal value proposition or brand helped give Sheila the confidence she needed to move forward and the courage to use the resource proclamation. It reminded her that she had the "right stuff," and she needed to use it to create an opportunity for people to "buy" her—because if that didn't happen, they most certainly would *not* buy the bank's products and services. It reminded her that she was "good enough," that she was promoted to the job because she was bright, talented, creative, and skillful. It will do the same things for you.

Second, describe yourself in terms of the outcomes you create, not the activities you engage in.

Next, make it your personal mission to always make others, including your boss, look good. Someone once said, "You can have anything you want; all you have to do is give others what they want." While there is the odd exception, to be sure, most people are fair and honest—willing to share credit where it's due. Making others look good sweeps you up in their success, and almost always guarantees that they will help you enjoy successes of your own.

Fourth, be a can-do person; take to heart the words of the old song, "The difficult I can do right now; the impossible will take a little while." Instead of saying, "I've never done that," say, "I'll learn how to do it." Don't be afraid of steep learning curves. Remember, the organization hired you because you were smart. Look for the opportunity in difficulties, rather than the difficulties in the opportunities.

Fifth, don't be afraid to fail or make mistakes. But if you do either, take responsibility—don't project or rationalize. Admitting a mistake or failure and moving forward is proactive, not reactive. Remember the Dale Carnegie adage:

> *Develop success from failures. Discouragement and failure are two of the surest stepping-stones to success. No other element can do so much for a man if he is willing to study them and make capital out of them.*

So, above all, identify and remember the learning opportunities in the situation. Forget about everything else and move on. There is no point in belaboring it or beating yourself up.

Sixth, ask for help. In my view, IQ expands exponentially—together, two people bring four times the intelligence. Superhero individualism is often counter productive. Remember, if you make others look good, they will be eager to do the same thing for you.

Seventh, remember the Pareto principle, or the 80/20 rule as it's more commonly known: eighty percent of your effectiveness comes from twenty percent of your activities. Manage your priorities, and don't waste time spinning your wheels by engaging unimportant activity.

Eighth, get yourself in front of an audience. Learn to make effective presentations, and make as many as you can. *Who knows what you know* is usually more important than what you know or who you know! Making sure that you, your ideas and skills receive broader corporate exposure can, in my experience, result in challenging new assignments, larger budgets, greater general recognition, and even raises and promotions.

Finally, develop and use internal and external networks, both formal and informal. People who network well often receive and move information faster, cut through organizational politics more quickly, and create solutions better suited to the needs of their companies. Research in different types of organizations shows that those who develop and use networks usually get to serve on more successful teams, receive early promotions more often, are more highly paid, and get better performance reviews.

Only nine—not quite a "top ten" list.

Whether you get ahead at work and in life is up to you. Go do it!

For many are called, but few are chosen:
Matthew 22:1

Tom Olson

Chapter Five

next week's newspaper

*If you don't know where you
are going, you can never get lost.*
—Herb Cohen

few years ago during a routine examination, my
physician and I began talking about our respective
stock market adventures and misadvetures— with
more emphasis on the latter, I might add. "Ah," she said, "If
only I had next week's newspaper…"

If only I had next week's newspaper. Interesting idea,
isn't it? Think of all the advantages of knowing what was
going to happen just one week in the future would bring: the
bets you'd win, the stock market killing you'd make… but
if you had next week's newspaper, would you read it all?
Would you read the obituaries? What if yours was among
them? Would you believe it? What would you do? Could you
change or stop history?

Have you ever thought about what it would be like to read your own obituary? And if you did get such advance notice, would do you think it would say? Would you be pleased? And if not, what would you do to change it?

Alfred Nobel, originator of the Nobel Peace Prize, did—in a manner of speaking. Inventing and manufacturing dynamite made Alfred Nobel a fabulously wealthy man. In 1888, when Alfred's brother, Ludvig, died while staying in Cannes, the French newspapers reported his death, but confused him with Alfred. One paper featured the headline, "Le Marchand de la Mort est Mort," or in *Anglais,* "The Merchant Of Death Is Dead."

Accidentally—or, perhaps, serendipitously—that sloppy editor triggered the thought and reflection that resulted Alfred's bequest for the Nobel Prizes and gave him an opportunity to change the impression people would have of him and his life after he died—to create a legacy much different from the one described by the confused editor. When he died eight years later, in 1896, Alfred left more than nine million dollars to fund awards for those whose work would benefit humanity, not destroy it. After reading his own obituary, then, he rewrote it to reflect this more positive remembrance, and then acted to ensure his legacy.

Writing an obituary that reflects a positive re-membrance is something we could all do—but how?

Well, start by writing your name at the top of a blank sheet of paper. Next, pick a fittingly bizarre way to die—crushed by stampeding elephants, overcome by dancing with Mick Jagger—anything but the usual causes. Pick a date far, far into the future—at least seventy-five to a hundred years (hey, with today's emerging medical technology, ninety-five will soon be a *premature* death).

Decide what you want your obituary to reflect: family, career, community service—whatever. The incorrect Nobel obituary reflected the downside of his business successes; the one he wrote himself concentrated on his humanitarian efforts. Create a priority list—family first, career second, community service third, and so on. Your obituary should reflect the focus of your current time and effort. If it doesn't, perhaps you should examine what you're doing and make some changes.

Then, decide what you've accomplished in life—not what you *will* have accomplished, but what you *have* accomplished. Taking an "accomplishment" view of your life clarifies where you want to go, and will help you to set long-term goals. Make your "accomplishments" as concrete, realistic, and achievable you can.

Define yourself in terms of what you are likely to accomplish, using either the resources at your disposal or the ones you can realistically acquire. Don't, for example, list "leading scorer in the National Hockey League in 2008" if you are over twenty-one and have never played hockey in your life! On the other hand, don't eliminate something like "became a physician and worked at developing a cure for male pattern baldness" if you truly still have the time and other resources needed to go to and graduate from medical school.

When you've finished writing your obituary, share it with someone close to you. Get that person to help make a plan for accomplishing all that's on your list. Then, put the obituary in a desk drawer. Take it out every so often just to check your progress. After a year or two, attach it to your Will and put it into a safety deposit box with instructions for publication in your local newspaper after your passing.

A very long, long time from now—and remember, live so the preacher doesn't have to lie at your funeral!

Writing our own obituary gives us a hypothetical peek into the future, but in some other respects, we actually *do* have a copy of next week's newspaper. Unfortunately, very few of us take the time to read it— we're just too bound up in today to pay attention to what's going to happen tomorrow. Often, we're too bound up in today to even think about yesterday. Most of us live in the moment.

All of this came to me at a swimming pool. We were vacationing in a hot spot and, because I'm an inveterate sun worshipper, I usually spend most of my time slathering my body with scented oils, baking by the pool, and spitting into the eyes of the gods of skin cancer.

On the second or third day of our vacation, as I was easing my sun-tortured body into a lounge chair, I noticed two incredibly attractive young people sharing a chaise lounge to the left of me. You know the types—sun streaked hair, great pecs, six-packs you could bounce cannonballs off, straight white teeth—bodies that were gravity defying in every way. People for whom mirrors are, as Martha Stewart would say, a good thing. And they were besotted with each other (although I had a sense that if someone had shown up with a mirror, each would have paid less attention to the other).

Afraid that all this beauty would blind me (and that someone would catch me staring), I averted my eyes and glanced in the other direction. What I saw there was plain *scary!* For slowly—very slowly—making their way to the pool, as though they were filing into God's waiting room, were a half-dozen or more *senior* citizens—really senior citizens. These people looked old enough to be the parents and grandparents of senior citizens!

They were all carrying large-print books; the effects of a lifelong struggle with gravity were clearly apparent, and if you were to fire a BB at any one of them, it would have gotten stuck in a mound of flaccid flesh or a wrinkle. Although they exchanged tender glances, it was clear the time of besottment was clearly long past.

What a contrast as I looked from left to right—the besotted and the liver-spotted. And there I was, in the middle: paunchy, a few laugh lines, growing a hole in my graying hair—somewhere between the two extremes that flanked me. Then it occurred to me—on my left was yesterday's newspaper, and on my right was tomorrow's—one headlining my lost youth, and the other the person I would become.

And I'd be willing to bet that, just as it never crossed my mind that I would sooner rather than later be part of the senior citizen set on my right, it didn't occur to the hard-bodied young couple that they would, one day, be middle-aged like me! The inability to recognize that, in my view, is neither unusual nor bad. None of us really believe we are going to get old (well, *that* old, anyway), and the realization that our time on earth is finite doesn't occur until very late in life.

We're caught in the moment, in our own context—so caught up in our day-to-day existence that we fail to notice what's happening around us.

Case in point: children. We rarely can imagine children being any older than they are at present (oh, maybe we can do intellectually, but it's a different story emo-tionally). When our children are five and eight, we're caught up with the problems, concerns, and joys of five and eight year olds. We don't project into the future wondering how we are going to deal with them at thirteen and sixteen. Similarly, we pay scant attention to what might occur when they are sixteen and nineteen.

We live in the present—and the present, we think, will last forever!

And that's okay. There's a certain futility that comes with growing older. Spending too much time thinking about where we'll all end up is to invite a sense of nihilism—and that, to paraphrase Martha again, is *not* a good thing! So, we spend a lot of time in our own context: thinking about where we are, not where we're going, as we almost unconsciously move through the stages from childhood to old age. We truly subscribe to the Buddhist admonition not to dwell in the past or dream of the future, but to concentrate the mind on the present moment.

The present becomes the past, however, and the future comes. We make the trip from besotted to liver spotted. And it's okay—getting older is better than the alternative.

So, what happens as we make the trip? Most of it is pretty predictable, according to lifespan psychologists. Regardless of where we're from, we spend our childhood in a small community—one populated by family, friends, teachers, coaches, church leaders, and others quite similar to us. In this small community we learn, in preparation for adulthood, the values and beliefs that define our character, mould our intellect, and influence our behaviour. In essence, childhood provides us with the tools for growing up.

At some point—usually in our late teens or early twenties—we pack up the tools and leave home (not for the first time, but for the last time) to make our way in the big bad world. Now, we don't call the big bad world the 'big bad world' for nothing! It can be a cold, demanding, and at times unforgiving place, and often there is little preparation for the initial shock of entry into it.

The transition from childhood to early adulthood usually tests long-held values and beliefs. Behaviours that were before considered acceptable are now ineffective or considered inappropriate. What is one to do? One choice made by many is to become 'kidults' or 'adultescents', and try to extend childhood indefinitely.

These people avoid the responsibilities and commitments of adult life, and extend adolescence well into their mid-to-late twenties; often they do not enter even a *provisional* stage of adulthood until their mid-thirties. Those in this group regard *Seinfeld* and *Friends* as reality television!

Another choice is to seriously consider becoming a functional adult at about the same age your parents did. Regardless of the choice you make, unless you are Peter Pan or one of his acolytes, that first step into adulthood is going to be a challenge. How do you cope? Well, over time, through a series of provisional tries, you reframe some of your values and beliefs, and take on new behaviours, while getting rid of those that are no longer effective or suitable.

As you work toward this restructured value-set and new behavioural repertoire, you begin to pick up some of the trappings of adult life: a car, a house, a spouse or partner, picket fence, spotted dog or striped cat, and perhaps even a child or two. You become an adult.

You settle in; life is good. You love your job, house, spouse, pets, cars, children, friends—everything. You're on cruise control. The feeling is often one of "If I knew it was going to be this good, I would have gotten here sooner." You can't wait for the next high-school reunion so people can see how wonderful you've become.

Yes, for many years, life is good! Then, one morning you wake up, roll over, gaze fondly at your husband, and suddenly realize you're married to your father-in-law— only thirty years younger. There he is—snoring softly, mouth agape, bits of drool rolling down his chin, hair falling out on the pillow, and suffering obvious gastrointestinal problems! You ask yourself, "What have I done?"

(Now, in fairness, men experience the same sort of phenomenon: there in bed lies a younger version of your mother-in-law, a vision in floor-length flannelette, snoring— but more softly; drooling—but with greater panache; suffering similar gastrointestinal problems— but in a more civilized fashion.)

Congratulations. You've entered the next, predictable stage of adulthood. (Some once called this age-thirty-crisis, but because of changed social dynamics, people now usually have these experiences at a later age.) You begin to ask, "Have I chosen the right career? Am I in the right job? Do I live in the right house? Do I have the right dog? Can I send my children back?"

This is not mid-life crisis—it's simply a period where you start to question all the decisions and choices you've made to this point in your adult life. It's where we often see a spate of personal change—bankers become poets, rock musicians become accountants, people divorce, careers change, moves take place to a different city or part of the world, and so on.

It's a difficult stage, but most people work through it. They stay married, solidify careers, and establish stronger relationships with their children. After that, little happens. You live for another thirty or forty years or so, and then you die.

"Oohhh, that's sooooo depressing," you might say. Well, depressing maybe, but true nonetheless. In truth, we're just bags of fertilizer that can walk, talk, and think. Death and taxes—both inevitable. Our time is finite. Honest acceptance of this places one firmly in mid-life.

Mid-life starts when you realize that you don't have enough time left to carry out all that you set out to do when you were younger. You aspired to the CEO's job, but at fifty-two, you're still in the mailroom. You're not going to get there. Nor are you going to build everything you wanted to build, travel to all the places you were going to travel. You simply are running out of time, and that's a very hard reality to face for many.

The crisis associated with this stage used to be almost the exclusive province of men, and the stereotypical response has often been one of younger women, faster cars, older whisky, and more money. Burned into our collective consciousness is the picture of a man in midlife trying to recapture his lost youth by driving off in a red two-seater with a woman half his age.

That happens, to be sure. But how many men *actually* do that? Very few, I would suggest. Most men and women (mid-life crisis is now a factor in the lives of women as well) deal with the crisis in a measured, healthy way, and as a result are able to work their way through it.

So, how do we deal with these various transitions and the structure-building periods between them? Simply knowing about and understanding the stage you are going through, and accepting it as part of normal, healthy adult development experienced simultaneously by many others certainly helps.

Control the process yourself. Think each experience through, examine your own reactions to them, and determine the extent to which they are effective or ineffective. Talk about the experience with your spouse, friends, and family. The more you feel in control, the less harmful the effects will be.

What happens after mid-life? Are there psycho-logical adventures yet to come for those who have successfully survived all the developmental stages? If there are, very little attention is currently being paid to them. But wait until the leading edge of the boomers reaches age sixty or so. Members of this generation—the most introspective and self-indulgent in history—have a high need to understand themselves. Look for an increase in interest, research, and publishing.

Write a book about it—not only will it probably make you rich; you could be a guest on Oprah, Letterman, and Leno! Meanwhile, enjoy the trip!

> *I still find each day too short for all the thoughts*
> *I want to think, all the walks I want to take, all the books I*
> *want to read, and all the friends I want to see.*
> —John Burroughs

Tom Olson

Chapter Six

of criminals and cousins

I know the price of success: dedication,
hard work, and an unremitting devotion
to the things you want to see happen.
—Frank Lloyd Wright

This may seem like an unusual thing for me to admit, but for a person in my position, I've know an inordinately large number of criminals.

Former criminals may be a more apt description. I think that most if not all of them have done their time in the Big House (a little B-movie terminology here for effect), and are now using their not-inconsiderable skills and talents to pursue more legitimate endeavors.

Now, you may have heard the "root cause" theory of criminal behaviour: in a nutshell, subscribers to this notion claim criminal behaviour is a product of poverty and lack of education, rather than simply individual disposition. In essence, bank robbers don't steal money because it beats working for it, but because their childhoods were unhappy. With enough therapy, supposedly, they will be able to come to grips with the true cause of their socially unacceptable behaviours and, as a result, cast them aside to engage in more salubrious pursuits.

This theory has gained great currency over the past twenty-five years or so. And although there may be some truth to it, it doesn't hold up in my experience. For, you see, all the criminals of my acquaintance— unlike many non-criminals—are from solid middle or upperclass backgrounds and often are university or college graduates. In fact, most of them have either law or business degrees!

In contrast, and surprisingly—if you're a root cause advocate— my *non*—criminal friends, even though they grew up in limited circumstances, have managed to overcome whatever early handicaps they may have had and went on to become productive members of our society. Along the way, many of them managed to amass some serious assets. So, forgive me if I question the "root cause" theory.

But I digress. Let me get back to my criminal friends (and mostly they *have* remained friends) for a moment. While they all tried to do well at their preferred types of criminality, in truth, they were abject failures. I mean, they all went to jail! That alone speaks volumes about their lack of competence. Collectively, these characters were more like the Gang That Couldn't Shoot Straight than the slick criminal operatives you see in the movies.

Now, although I'd never suggest choosing a career in crime to anybody, I do believe whatever you do, you should do it to the best of your ability—and these guys (I don't know any female criminals) had abundantability. With all they had going for them, why were they such bad criminals?

I think part of the answer is found in the company they kept. They hung out with other criminals, most of whom were, at best, mediocre —people with names like Jimmy the Booster and Lucky the Lip, all of whom had room temperature IQs and wore their bad habits and stupidity like badges of honour. And the longer my well-brought up, well-educated friends hung around these criminal characters, the more like them they became— they drank too much, became drug-dependent, took bad risks, and made poor decisions. It was though the side of their heads had cracked and allowed whatever brain cells they hadn't managed to kill to leak out. Over time, they lowered their expectations and standards until they became indistinguishable from the others in their criminal circles.

If they really wanted to be good criminals, these friends of mine would have sought out the company of successful criminals: those who enjoy their ill-gotten gains and stay out of the slammer longer (more B-movie talk). Why? Because if you work and play with people who are better than you are at something, by associ-ating with them regularly, you'll become better yourself. (Oh, by the way—I really don't believe there are suc-cessful criminals, just some who stay out of jail for a little longer than others).

Has anybody ever said his (or her) game suffered because they played with Wayne Gretzky or Natalie Gulbis? *Au contraire*—those who have played with them invariably report becoming better players because of the experience of playing alongside these exceptional athletes.

Why? Because they had to raise their expectations, and maximize their abilities to play up to the calibre of these more accomplished athletes. In short, successful people raise the bar, and they challenge one to be better. They create environments in which there is no room for mediocrity.

There are people who prefer mediocrity, often because it's much easier to succeed or feel successful in a mediocre world than it is to achieve in an environment of excellence. And just as success breeds more success, mediocrity breeds more mediocrity; and, as a result, success in a mediocre world is often short-lived, because people in that world want nothing more than company, and they will drag others down to their level as quickly as they can. So, spend your time with successful people. It's energizing. It's fun. You'll learn what it takes to be successful, and more importantly, what you need to do to maintain that success.

And who are these successful people? Well, that depends largely on your definition of success. On a personal basis, there are likely almost as many definitions of success as there are people in the world. There is material success, of course but there is also academic, spiritual, marital, athletic, philosophical, physical, parental, and many other types to consider. How you define success is less important than what you do to attain and maintain it. I firmly believe that anyone can be successful—even those who have grown up in difficult circumstances, or who suffer seemingly overwhelming obstacles or difficulties later in life.

Woody Allen once claimed that eighty percent of success is showing up. While that may contain a kernel of truth, I'd change it ever so slightly —but, I think, significantly—to *"eighty percent of success is showing up thinking that you can be successful."*

My cousin Beverley is a case in point. Slim and attractive, Beverley is a very successful insurance broker in the United Kingdom. She is a member of the *Million Dollar Round Table,* an industry group whose members comprise the top sales professionals in the life-insurance based financial services business. Her membership in this exclusive industry club has provided her with a large measure of professional respect and recognition, as well as the opportunity to attend MDRT-sponsored meetings and conferences throughout the world. In fact, as I write this, she is traveling home from three weeks in the Far East. By just about any measure, she is an unqualified success. However, it wasn't always so.

My first meeting with cousin Beverley was on the telephone during the reunion party we held for my mother and her siblings. In our brief conversation, I learned that she was a single mother of two teenage boys who, after her marriage collapsed, moved from the east side of England to Chepstow, a small city in Wales. Before I "rang off," as they say in the UK, I invited her and the boys to come and stay with us should they ever get to North America.

When I extend invitations like that, my wife shud-ders! "Nothing to worry about," I said. "She's a single mother with two teenage boys, limited resources, and a job I'm sure hardly pays enough to make ends meet. What are the chances?"

Beverley and the boys arrived on our doorstep the following summer, and it was one of the best things that ever happened to us! Whatever apprehension we may have had about their visit immediately vanished upon meeting her and the boys. Beverley was, and is, outgoing, upbeat, adventuresome, and unfailingly optimistic—a joy to be around. Her boys were, and are, smart, active, friendly, responsible, and polite.

Since that first meeting, the two families have combined to make close to thirty transatlantic trips to visit one another. But, until I screwed up the courage to ask her, the question that hounded me was, "How did she manage to get here? Single mother, two boys, just starting out in a brand-new line of work, much responsibility and little money. *How?*"

When, several years after that first visit, I finally asked, here, in a nutshell, is what she told me. "During our first telephone conversation, you said if I ever came to North America, I was to stay with you. When I rang off, the first thought I had was, '*when* I go to North America, I shall stay with Tom and his family.' That's the first step—determining what success means to you—defining it, writing down and then describing what the successful condition will look like.

"When I speak of the future and what I want to do, I always say *when*, never *if*. To say *if* lessens the degree of confidence one has about achieving something. It also implies greater reliance on events happening by chance rather than by one's own efforts. So I say *when*. *When* implies a goal, and when I have a clear goal, I can set a deadline for achieving it and start creating a plan. Once all that's in place, all I need to do is work the plan."

"And you do that consistently, for everything?" I asked.

"Absolutely," she replied. "For instance, when I started in the insurance business, I didn't say, *if* I become a member of the Million Dollar Round Table, I'll be able to do this and that. I said *when* I become a member, this is what it will look like, and this is what I'll be able to do. Goal, deadline, plan— it's not rocket science."

"But it can't work *every* time, surely!" I exclaimed. "I mean, what about early on, after your marriage broke up and you were left on your own? There must have been times when your confidence ebbed, when nothing worked, when you felt life was conspiring against you, and the future was too bleak to even think about."

"Oh, I never regarded the future as being bleak," Beverley replied. "Rather, I took the position that the future is mine to create. Of course there were difficulties, but I took the position that it was my responsibility to overcome them.

"It would have been easy to fall into the trap of thinking of myself in the way many in this world would like single mothers to be characterized—weak, at risk, unable to fend for themselves, in need of a plethora of government and therapeutic support. But I didn't believe that I was either powerless or a victim of circumstances outside my control. I don't now, nor did I then, believe that I was incapable of dealing with life's difficulties and challenges on my own. Rather, I was, and am, a robust, independent Kentish woman, capable of achieving all sorts of great successes. And it all starts with deciding what I'm to do, saying when, setting a deadline, and creating and working a plan."

"Okay, okay," I said, "I'm beginning to get it. The message is pretty consistent—goal, deadline, plan, execute—I can do that! But I'm interested about the deadline stuff. I mean, how do you determine your time frames for achievement, and why is having a deadline so important?" She was very patient with me: "A dream without a deadline is still a dream. A dream with a deadline is a goal! You have to have an end point—it focuses your efforts, and stops you from procrastinating and doing other, low-priority stuff. I also believe you should let people know what your goals are, and when you expect to achieve them."

"Isn't that a little risky?" I ventured. "There's a great deal of personal exposure in doing that. What if you fail? Aren't you worried about what people would say?"

"I'd rather have them say 'she failed' than 'she didn't try.' Everybody fails in something sometime. The only people who don't fail are those who don't try. But all of that aside, the fact that I've told other people what I'm going to do means they will hold me accountable—I'm actually going to have to 'walk my talk,' so to speak. It acts as an incentive.

When it comes to time frames, it is most important that they are realistic. Rome, as they say, wasn't built in a day. Some goals are going to take longer to achieve than others. For those goals with a long time frame, I make sure I have some intermediate objectives and some mileposts so I can measure my progress. I move in increments and, without exception, I celebrate each incremental achievement. Success encourages success."

Like most successful people, at the beginning of her journey, Beverley recognized that she needed the help and efforts of others to be successful. She sought out and associated with people who modeled what, in her mind, she needed to learn to move forward. And learn she did. Successful people, along with their penchant for goal setting and taking personal responsibility for their own outcomes, have plenty of other characteristics and behaviours that set them apart from the less accomplished Beverley discovered.

And what are these characteristics and behaviours that set successful people apart? What is it these people   we should seek out and hang around with do? Well, according to Beverley, successful people have a creative vision they support with well articulated values and beliefs that guide their actions, both daily and in the long term. Their focus is not simply solving problems, but on producing results that matter or make a positive difference to themselves and others.

They expect more of themselves and those around them. They have high standards and will not tolerate half measures. They value their resources and maximize their use. They focus on and are committed to achieving what they set out to do. They stay the course. To use a sports analogy, they give 110 percent, emptying the tank every day.

Like everyone else, successful people make mistakes—the difference is in how they handle them. When they make a mistake, they admit it, analyze what happened, pull together a plan, apologize, and change their strategy. In other words, to use a popular expression, they deal with it! They regard failure as a learning opportunity, realizing the only time you don't fail is the last time you do something and it works.

They wake up excited, and their enthusiasm is infectious. To them, the glass is always half-full, and today is sure to be better than yesterday. Their personal energy shows excitement about what they are doing, and confidence that they are making a difference.

They show interest in other opinions and points of view. Their communication mantra is "ask, listen, respond." They are willing to change their own opinion if the facts warrant doing so. They are respectful without being obsequious. Successful people do not "suck up." They are tolerant without being relativistic. They accept another's right to hold a different opinion, value, or belief, but will not subscribe to the notion that all opinions, values, or beliefs have equal weight. They will stand up for their own beliefs and values, even when they run counter to popular opinion.

They are unfailingly kind. They show up when they're needed. They give of themselves: their time, money, ideas, and whatever else might contribute to their communities. Many tithe, and almost all volunteer.

Successful people use the language well. Recognizing there is power in language, they build their vocabularies—not for the sake of using fifty-dollar words to describe fifty-cent ideas, but for the ability to express themselves with greater clarity. They use the language of success, avoiding the negative and the nihilistic, preferring to speak positively, read positive literature, and listen to confidence building messages. They regard negative feedback as an opportunity to learn and grow, and they present negative feedback in positive ways. They accept positive feedback graciously.

Finally, they put everything in perspective. They look for and create balance in their lives. They realize that success is far more than simple acquisition of money and the other overt symbols normally associated with success.

In the words of my cousin Beverley: "Oh, it's not about the money! Don't get me wrong —the money's important, but it's not what gets me up in the morning. It's the sense of accomplishment, knowing that I've overcome a few obstacles and achieved some really significant successes, at work and with my friends and family. It's about being recognized by my peers, and getting to associate with the most successful people in business and life. It's about having the opportunity to learn from the best what it takes to be the best, and what it takes to continue to be the best.

"But, just as nothing succeeds like success, nothing recedes like success. I've found that staying here may actually be harder than getting here was, so I still say when, set a deadline, and create a plan."

> *To laugh often and much; to win the respect of intelligent people and the affection of children; to earn the appreciation of honest critics and endure the betrayal of false friends; to appreciate beauty, to find the best in others; to leave the world a little better; whether by a healthy child, a garden patch or a redeemed social condition; to know even one life has breathed easier because you have lived. This is the meaning of success.*
> —Ralph Waldo Emerson

Chapter Seven

the pedantic podiatrist and Martin Luther King

*No one can make you feel
inferior without your consent.*
—Eleanor Roosevelt

*A guy walks into a podiatrist's office and says,
"Doc, you gotta help me! I think I'm a moth!"
The doctor says, "You don't need a podiatrist.
You need a psychiatrist.
What did you come in here for?"
"Well, your light was on..."*

I've never been to a podiatrist—probably wouldn't drop in, even *if* his light was on!—although I've a friend who goes to one regularly. His toenails are like clamshells—impossible to trim using normal, from-the -drugstore-to-your-bathroom-type clippers. So, whenever he feels his burgeoning pedodigits are threatening his shoe leather, off he goes to his podiatrist (who I suspect uses hedge trimmers).

And when he goes for his for onychogryphosis and/ or onychomycosis treatments (the reason podiatry is a four year program is that it takes three years to learn how to spell these words, and another one to figure out how to pronounce them!), my friend delights in the pleasures and pleasantness of the podiatric pampering—but for one thing. His podiatrist never shuts up. A non-stop talker, he starts before he removes the first sock, and doesn't quit until he sweeps away the last of the toenail shavings and/or foot-fungus remnants, and collects his fee.

Now I'm sure the podiatrist—like many other medical service providers—has taken a few courses that teach about engaging clients in witty and urbane conversation while heaping indignities on various parts of their anatomy, and that's good. But this podiatrist is not a conversationalist—he's a talker. And what does he talk non-stop about? His political values and religious beliefs—values and beliefs that, as it turns out, are diametrically opposed to those of my friend!

And what does my friend do when the podiatrist is pontificating? He grows increasingly uncomfortable! And what does he say to the pontificating podiatrist? Absolutely nothing! Why? He doesn't want to argue with a man holding hedge clippers in his hand!

In truth, he stays quiet because he really doesn't know how to tell the podiatrist, in an appropriate way, that he disagrees with him. So, hoping to avoid confrontation, he stays quiet. He leaves with his stomach in a knot, vowing that next time—if there is a next time (and there always is)—he'll speak up.

He never does, which only makes the encounter worse. Because my friend doesn't voice his opinion or disagreement, the podiatrist thinks they are both on the same page! So, the podiatrist's verbosity increases, as does my friend's frustration.

Sound familiar?

Probably. Most people have been caught in similar situations. The circumstances may be different, but the outcomes are the same—knotted stomach, frustration, anger, and promises to never engage with that person or group of people again. One usually reneges on the vow, however, and the whole exasperating experience repeats again and again.

All of this provides a classic example of the effects of passive behaviour. Reacting passively and allowing the needs, opinions, and judgments of others to become more important than your own usually results in feelings of anxiety, hurt, and anger. And, because deep down we know that passive behaviour is emotionally dishonest and self-denying, we are often more upset with ourselves than we are with the other person.

To quell these feelings of discomfort, we need to break the cycle of passivity, express our ideas and feelings, and let others know what we think and believe in a measured, intelligent way—have an intelligent, objective discussion, if you like.

In today's world, however, where affect seemingly always overrides objectivity, there seems to be very little room for civilized, meaningful discourse. Instead, we have shouting, labeling, and overt expressions of how one "feels" about an issue. Often, one is called a "left-wing commie whacko," "right wing weirdo," "homophobe," "tree hugger," "fascist," or any other of a multitude of labels, for simply disagreeing with certain popularly held opinions. You can find ample evidence of the decline of civilized debate simply by tuning your television to legislative question periods or crossfire.

When conversations turn to any one of the many contentious, politically correct issues that abound today, the problem is exacerbated. Often, any effort to encourage or start meaningful debate around one of these issues results in accusations that one is intolerant and/or judgmental. People are incredibly afraid of being labeled in these ways so they avoid any discussion of their beliefs. Ironically, while many of the accusers claim to value tolerance most highly, they are often the ones who, in my experience, will not tolerate any questioning of, or disagreement with, blind acquiescence to their politically correct notions!

As a result, we have a culture within which, in the words of Martin Luther King.

Many people fear nothing more terribly than to take a position that stands out sharply and clearly from the prevailing opinion. The tendency of most is to adopt a view that is so ambiguous that will include everything, and so popular that it will include everybody. Not a few men who cherish loyalty and noble ideals hide them under a bushel for fear of being called different.

But should we be afraid of being called different? Does questioning a popular notion or disagreeing with a widely held opinion automatically make one intolerant or judgmental? Clearly not! But many people would rather suffer the knotted stomach and continuing frustration than risk standing up for what they think or believe or, even worse, give up and adopt the relativist position that all points of view have equal validity.

That, I think is a shame, for to paraphrase G.K. Chesterton and at least one country-and-western song, if you don't stand for something, you'll fall for everything. You need to be clear on what you value, and you need to communicate that to others—even when it seems that to do so would put you at risk.

Well-articulated, clearly defined, and effectively communicated values are essential to personal and professional effectiveness. They comprise the principles and beliefs that guide behaviour on a daily basis. If you truly value honesty, you will choose to be demonstrably honest always. If you value family strongly, you will make time for family a priority. If personal growth is a top value for you, you will make decisions that encourage personal development. Our values are the foundation-blocks upon which we build our lives.

How do we know when a value is a value? Seven criteria need to be met when defining a value. These are:

1. You choose the value freely without force or coercion.
2. You choose it from an array of alternatives.
3. You choose it after careful consideration of the consequences of holding it.
4. Holding this value brings happiness.
5. You act upon it.
6. You demonstrate behaviour that supports the value repeatedly and consistently; and, for me, most importantly,
7. *You publicly affirm that you hold this value.*

Note: the final criterion does not say it is publicly affirmed that this value is no better than any other; it says that *you* publicly affirm that you hold this. Implicit in this is that, *for you,* the value in question is superior to others—that *for you,* it is right. To be successful and effective, unless you receive convincing evidence to the contrary, you have to hold, and if necessary defend, the position that your values are absolutely the best ones to have.

Do not, in the face of bluster and bombast, shrink from that position. Now, I'm not suggesting that you have to argue your position. Simply saying "I don't agree with that," or "I have another point of view" will often diffuse uncomfortable or potentially incendiary situations, and turn the conversation to something more amenable to good fellowship.

Quietly stating what you believe often has the same effect. For example, at a dinner party I recently attended, one guest, using the approach of the aforementioned podiatric pedant, went on a rant about religion—loudly and unequivocally expressing several uninformed and unsubstantiated opinions. I was quite uncomfortable with what he was saying, as were some of the other guests. When he took a breath to reload, I quietly interjected, saying, "While I respect your right to hold those opinions, we're a faith based family and I believe in God."

End of rant—he didn't react angrily or defensively—he just stopped talking about it! I didn't have to explain my position, and nor would I, had I been asked.

In my view, most human behaviour that we find objectionable is unintended. My fellow dinner guest didn't really intend to make anybody uncomfortable with his comments—he simply assumed, wrongly, that everyone at the table was of an opinion similar to his. Had I not let him know that I, for one, disagreed, he would have continued with his rant, and the other guests would have kept squirming in their chairs. Instead, after ten seconds or so of subdued silence, the conversation turned to something of mutual interest that we could all talk about comfortably.

There are those who would say I should have posed a more strenuous challenge and required that he justify his statements while trying to influence him to my view. While there might be some merit to this, I felt a dinner party was neither the time nor place to engage in a heated discussion about something as profoundly personal as religious belief. Besides, in this instance, if he's right, it doesn't make any difference. But if I'm right, for him anyway, there could be hell to pay!

Anyway, although I don't agree with his views, I will fight to the death for his right to express them freely. And as I respect his views, so should he respect mine. Neither of us, however, has the right to impose our own beliefs or views on the other. Do we have the responsibility to try to influence each other to our respective positions? I would say yes, but only in a measured, reasoned, and objective discussion, in the proper place, and at the proper time.

And how does one do that?

Assertively.

Assertive people are clear about their agenda, and express their rights without violating the rights of others. They communicate in a manner that is suitably direct, open, honest, and self-enhancing. They have no qualms about letting others know what they stand for and what they are looking for. Their verbal and non-verbal behaviours imply confidence and strength. While respecting the other person, assertive people describe behaviours and their impacts, rather than affix labels, and use "I" statements ("I want…" / "I need…") to request the changes they see as necessary.

Acting assertively heightens your sense of self-confidence and will usually gain you the respect of others. It increases the potential for honest relationships, and helps you to feel better about your ability to control everyday situations—which, in turn, improves your decision-making, and your chances of getting what you really want from life. Acting assertively means you recognize that you have some fundamental rights, and that you are willing to defend them if needed.

What are these rights? And, apart from accepting that these rights extend to everybody, not just you, what *responsibilities* come with them?

While you have the right to your own values, beliefs, and opinions, regardless of the opinion of others, you also have the responsibility to "walk the talk"—to model consistently the behaviours implied by what you espouse. You also have the responsibility to examine continually and think critically about what you value and believe. You have the right to decide how to lead your life, make your own decisions, pursue your own goals, and establish your own priorities, but with that right comes the responsibility for marshalling the resources you need, and accepting both the positive and negative consequences of your decisions and actions.

You have the right to make a mistake, but the responsibility for getting the information or help you need to avoid making the same mistake again. While you have the right to tell others what you expect from them and how you wish to be treated, you have the responsibility of expressing those expectations in clear, unequivocal terms.

Except as required under law, you have the right to refuse to justify or explain your actions or feelings to others—but you have the responsibility to "own" those actions and feelings. You have the right to express yourself, but the responsibility to do so in a way that is not offensive to others. You have the right to take time to develop your ideas before expressing them, but the responsibility to respect the other person's need for information and answers.

While you have the right to have positive, satisfying personal and professional relationships, within which you feel comfortable and are free to express yourself, you have the responsibility for doing the work that you have to do to maintain them. You have the right to change or end relationships if they don't meet your needs, but you have the responsibility for describing the nature and location of the "gaps" in these relationships and taking proactive actions to close them. You have the right to change, enhance, or develop your life in any way you decide, but not at the expense of others.

Proclaiming and standing up for these rights is not selfish, but demanding rights without accepting the accompanying responsibilities, or showing concern about your rights only, with little or no regard for others, is. When you are selfish in these matters or behave in a way that violates the rights of others, rather than acting in a constructive, assertive manner, you are, in fact, demonstrating destructive, aggressive behaviour.

Many people confuse assertiveness and aggressiveness ; a very fine line divides the two types of behaviour. Aggressive people express their rights, but at the expense, degradation, or humiliation of others. They use emotional and/or physical force to limit or squash the rights of others. Aggressiveness often results in feelings of anger, vengefulness, and loss of respect; is counter-productive; and not a strategy I'd recommend.

It is okay, though, to use assertive behaviours to aggressively pursue your goals. How can you become more assertive?

Start by communicating what you want, think, and feel with clarity and precision. When you're feeling ambiguous, say "I have mixed reactions to this. This is what I agree with, and here are the reasons why I'm concerned about other parts." If you disagree or have a different opinion, simply say, "I have a different view, I believe that…"

When providing feedback, whether on something that was done well or something you want changed, describe the behaviour in question, its impact on you, and what you'd like the other to do to change or maintain the behaviour. It's usually helpful to explain exactly what you mean and what you don't mean. For example, if you have an issue with a co-worker, you might say, "My purpose here is not to criticize, but to get to the root of this problem and decide what we need to do to prevent it from happening again." Finally, if there is something you want, don't beat around the bush; begin by saying, "I want…".

Next, if you want to tell somebody something, tell him or her directly, preferably in person. If you want to tell me something, tell me directly; do not tell everyone except me; do not tell a group of which I happen to be a member. *Tell me.* That way, there'll be no confusion about the message.

Acknowledge that your message comes from your frame of reference by using personalized "I" statements, such as "I don't agree with you," rather than "You're wrong." Use strong, confident voice tones, gestures, eye contact, facial expression, and posture.

Finally, ask for feedback: "Am I being clear?" "Are we both seeing this from the same angle?" "What do you want to do?" "Is what I'm doing consistent with your expectations?" Getting feedback enables you to correct any misperceptions or misconceptions you may have, and helps others realize you are expressing an opinion, feeling, or wish, rather than a demand. Encourage others to be clear, direct, and specific in their feedback to you.

When you allow the needs, opinions, and judgments of others to become more important than your own, you are likely to feel hurt, anxious, and even angry. This passive or nonassertive behaviour is often indirect, emotionally dishonest, and self-denying.

Asserting yourself will not necessarily guarantee intelligent discussion, happiness, or fair treatment by others—nor will it solve all your personal problems, or guarantee that others will be less aggressive. Being assertive does not mean you will always get what you want; however, lack of assertiveness will most certainly guarantee that you don't.

The ultimate measure of a man is not where he stands in moments of comfort, but where he stands at times of challenge and controversy.
—Martin Luther King Jr.

Tom Olson

Chapter Eight

the garage door's half up

*The point of living and of being
an optimist is to be foolish enough
to believe the best is yet to come.*
—Peter Ustinov

I am not a big fan of popular culture. Except for sporting events and the odd program on PBS, I've stopped watching television. In recent years, the only movies I've seen in a theatre were *Polar Express* and *Madascar*. If a piece of fiction wins a literary award of any type, except in unusual circumstances, I go out of my way not to read it. Why? Because there is little—perhaps nothing—in television, movies, and literature that is noble, uplifting, encouraging, redeeming, or optimistic! Quite the contrary. If you want to confirm any suspicions you may have about our society being made up of mostly sick, evil, depressed, stressed, conspiratorial, suicidal, sexually deviant, abusive, violent, satanic, nihilistic, existential people who are all essentially victims of personal, familial, corporate, religious, military, government, or extraterrestrial abuse, go to a movie or pick up a book.

Rarely is there anything heroic in movies or literature. If heroism shows up at all, movies and books present it as heroic suffering rather than heroic achievement. Audiences are required to identify with and admire the sufferers. We are asked to believe that those who can accept and live with whatever pain has been foisted on them, usually by forces outside their control, are heroic and more worthy of applause than those who risk jousting with and destroying those same forces for the sake of making the world better. Being able to *"take it"* is more heroic than *"doing something about it."*

The blue-and-gray lighting and the grim counte-nances of the pasty-faced characters in most television dramas imply that we live in some hellish underworld. We're shown lurid, gory, violent murders, followed by depictions of autopsies so detailed that they could be used as instructional videos for coroners in training!

With the odd exception, television comedy provides little more than the sex and bathroom humour characteristic of college sophomores.

What about newspapers and television news? There are no better places to find unbalanced overkill than these two media. The tragedy du jour dominates newspaper headlines and the top of the news on television— SARS, Mad Cow disease, road rage, killer bees, shark attacks, global warming, skin cancer, tainted tuna, terrorist attacks, West Nile Virus, and God knows how many other "imminent risks" to life on the planet have been given huge coverage in recent years.

These stories are presented with great drama and with considerable gravity—the anchors and editors emphasize the risk to human health and well being while downplaying (or omitting altogether) any information that puts that risk in perspective. Mad Cow disease is a case in point. Based on available figures, to kill the same number as was projected to die of influenza in 2004, Americans would have to eat about two billion BSE-infected cows—about ten mad cows per adult. Only four or five BSE-infected cows have been found in North America. Because the only way a cow can get BSE from another infected cow is by eating it, there is no chance of a BSE epidemic. Rules recommended by the World Health Organization and imposed in Canada, the United States, and all Western nations in recent years forbid the use of cow feed containing material from other ruminants. Bet you didn't hear that on your local television news broadcast.

But what's the reality? The reality is that things *really aren't all that bad.* Proportionately, fewer people are hungry or sick today than were one hundred years ago; infant mortality has dropped to a record low, and life expectancy has reached a record high. We have a full hour more of free time each day than in 1965. Personal disposable income has tripled in the past fifty years. Cancer death rates are declining. The Third World is getting richer, and even the most oppressed are living longer than they did even fifty years ago.

So, why are we wallowing in this pool of skepticism, cynicism, and pessimism?

At one time, we were a much more optimistic society, given to celebrating human achievement, and making positive predictions about the future. Our forebears had tamed the wilderness, and fought off oppressors in two wars. Medical research was developing vaccines and procedures to all but eliminate diseases that had previously killed millions. Scientists developed technology that provided us a lifestyle unimaginable as recently as the beginning of twentieth century.

Our cultural story was one of inner strength, self-reliance, and great individual and collective achievement—a story that emphasized human successes at overcoming personal, medical, and environmental hardship. There was a shared confidence that our social, political, and religious institutions would carry us successfully into the future—a confidence that we had the stuff necessary to make true Wilfred Laurier's early twentieth-century assertion that "Canada... is only commencing.... Canada will fill the twentieth century."

Early in the twenty-first century, most people would scoff at Laurier's claim. Many see our political, social, and religious institutions as incapable of shaping the future. Conspiracy theories—concerned with the evil intentions of business, government, and religion to strip us of our rights, and control every aspect of our lives— abound. We have revised our story so it no longer celebrates human achievement, but emphasizes the environmental and social damage done as we've moved forward in history.

In a nutshell, it tells us that we've screwed up the past, the present isn't all that great, we're incapable of securing the future, and there's nothing we can do about it! The world is spinning out of control and we're all headed for hell in a hand basket, so the story goes.

Collectively and individually, we are fragile and powerless, subject to the vagaries of forces outside our control. There are no viable alternatives, and our ineffective institutions limit our individual and collective ability to change conditions and events. We might as well accept our fate—in short, we're hooped!

Perhaps the most effective propaganda technique used in Nazi Germany was that of the "Big Lie"— repeating something so loudly and persistently that people began believing it. I think the "Big Lie" approach is being used again—this time, to perpetuate the notion that people in today's society cannot cope with or face the big challenges of life on their own. That everyone is essentially helpless.

I don't buy it—I don't think anybody should. I believe the world is a better place than it has been in the past, and will become an even better place in the future. My answer to the phenomenological question "How are you today?" is "Great! I woke up this morning—after that, it just gets better!"

I'm an inveterate optimist. I tend to see the positive aspects of situations, and to anticipate positive outcomes. I prefer to hang out with people who share similar perspectives.

Why?

Because my optimistic friends *make things happen.* They focus on how to get things done, rather than on why they can't be done. They set ambitious goals and commit to their achievement. They are both persistent and resilient—there is no challenge or problem that can't be overcome, and they have the staying power to be successful regardless of how long it takes.

These folks generally have high self-esteem and display a refreshing self-confidence. They expect to be successful—and more often than not, are. Each success increases their expectation of future success, and on those rare occasions where they suffer setbacks or rejection, they tend to bounce back quickly.

They have a strong internal locus of control. Because they feel they can influence and control the events in their lives, they tend to try harder. When the going gets tough, they have the attitudes and skills needed to manage their motivation—and, as a result, they are often more productive than pessimists or those less optimistic. They don't quit.

Because they regard change as an opportunity, they generally cope better with new circumstances or a changing environment. They tend to be healthier and live longer. Finally, they usually display a palpable energy—one that others can feed off and be motivated by. That, along with the other aforementioned characteristics, is why I prefer their company to that of the doom-and-gloom and professional-pessimist crowds.

Now, don't get me wrong. I am not a blind, delusional Pollyanna, living in a fantasy world where bad stuff never happens; nor, although generally very positive, am I an advocate of the "If you can't be positive here, be negative somewhere else!" school of thought. I recognize there is a place for pessimism, and have little patience with the almost infantile assumption of positive thinking that we can create our own destiny simply by using the powers of our mind and repeating positive statements to ourselves.

The place for pessimism? When a real risk of a severe, life-threatening or life-damaging negative consequence exists, a cautious, risk-avoiding approach makes good sense. But when the risk is small (some wasted time and effort, a little public embarrassment, the possibility of several failures before success), better to take the optimistic view and act!

Unlike positive thinking, optimism depends on and is embedded in reality and action. Optimism works not through an unrealistic and unjustifiable positive view of how the world works, but through the power of "non-negative" thinking. An optimist does not repress or ignore negative thoughts, but instead *reframes* them in a systematic way that better conforms to the reality of the situation, and gives them greater psychological usefulness.

I found the statement "My mother made me an optimist" written on a restroom wall when I was in graduate school. Below it was written, "If I give her some wool, do you think she could make me one, too?"

Well, my mother didn't make me an optimist, but the mother of friends did. Allison Monahan—Jim and Sharon's mother—was a burn-unit nurse who dealt daily with some of the most distressing medical situations imaginable. Yet, like many others in her profession, she maintained a positive, optimistic outlook— something I'm sure she passed along to her patients.

Allison was both my biggest fan and my mother confessor—the person to whom I would go when I felt I couldn't talk to my own parents about something. Most of what I talked to her about was the somewhat pervasive sense of inadequacy many young people feel.

Her responses to my difficulties were pretty consistent. I would credit my difficulty with school to my lack of brains, and she would say, "You just need a better tutor." When I said we won a baseball game because the other team played poorly, she responded with, "You won because you played really well tonight." I would bemoan my lack of interpersonal skills, and she would tell me that, "So-and-so is a very difficult person to get along with." When I complained that I would never get a summer job, she would say, "The competition for jobs is tough, but if you keep trying, you're sure to find something."

And on it went—I would moan about the hopelessness of whatever situation I'd found myself in, and my feelings of helplessness about bringing it to resolution. Allison would reframe my self-pitying comments and try to get me to look at things from a different angle. Finally, one night when I was in full whine, she looked at me and said, "Tommy, I'm tired of propping you up. You have a STD, and we need to find a cure and get you over it!"

A STD! I was shocked, and just a little scared—after all, I didn't think you could get one of those on your own.

"A STD?" I asked tentatively—"What kind of STD, and can I get a shot for it?"

"Stinkin' Thinkin' Disorder!" she replied. "And yes, you can get a shot—but you have to give it to yourself. You have to change how you think and talk about both the positive and negative things that happen. I've tried to give you some examples, but it's time you started getting it done on your own."

Man, was I glad for the STD explanation, but I have to admit that I was still a little confused. "What do you mean, I have to change how I think and talk about things?"

"Well, look at the way you explain the things that happen to you," she said. "If you win, you say it was luck; if you fail, you say it's because you're stupid; things 'always' or 'never' happen to you. When you hit a rough patch, you assume that it's your fault, that it will last forever, and that it will work against or undermine everything you do. You react as though you are helpless to do anything about it. You don't challenge any of these beliefs."

"Do not! Do so!" I replied, more than a little defensively.

Ignoring my feeble protest, she continued, "What you have to do is react to setbacks from the position that you're in charge—that you have the power to make things better. You need to start telling yourself that bad events are just temporary setbacks, specific to particular circumstances, and that they can be overcome by your own effort and abilities. If you change how you think, you'll change how you feel!"

"And then what?" I asked.

"Take credit for your successes. Success is not an accident—it's the result of hard work. Next time you do something well, tell yourself, 'I did well because I'm good at that', or 'my hard work sure paid off.' And remember, there are no tough times, only tough people."

Now, all of this sounded fine in theory, but how was I supposed to challenge my thinking on a day-to-day basis? How could I train myself to recognize when my thinkin' was stinkin'? What could I do to dispute it and turn it around?

Her answer was nothing short of brilliant.

"What would you do if some stranger called you a loser, a wimp, or something else like that?" she asked. "You'd defend yourself, wouldn't you? You'd say, 'you're wrong', and then provide a list of reasons why. Treat your stinkin' thinkin' in the same way you would treat an insult from somebody else—defend yourself, and give reasons why it's wrong—because your 'stinkin thinkin' is an insult. When you do it, you are insulting yourself!

"When something is going wrong, listen to the messages you're giving yourself about why things aren't working out the way you want—write them down if you can. How are you explaining the setback to yourself? Identify how these explanations are affecting your energy, emotions, willingness to act, and so on. Write all of this down, and then read it aloud to yourself.

"Pick the messages apart, just as you'd pick apart a comment about being a loser—challenge their usefulness. Generate alternative specific, external, and temporary explanations for why things are not going well. Focus on evidence that contradicts or undermines your negative explanations and supports a more positive interpretation."

She took an elastic band from a kitchen drawer and put it around my wrist. "Leave this on all the time, even in the bath," she said. "When it wears out, replace it with a new one. Use it when you become overwhelmed with negative thoughts or worries. Snap it on your wrist and holler, 'Stop!' Make a note of what's getting in the way, and set a time to think about it in the future. And then move on and deal with the difficulty at hand."

Now, I have to admit all of this was a little overwhelming. It sounded easy, but I was sure it wasn't. And I was right.

It worked, however. Not overnight, to be sure; in fact, it took years and much mental discipline. It was an investment, and as with any good investment strategy, I started small, did it consistently and intelligently over time, and let the magic of compounding do its work. And then, in time, almost without my realizing it, my default response to setbacks became one of optimism rather than pessimism.

I am richer for the experience—learning and applying the mechanics of optimism has enabled me to create healthier and more accurate alternatives to thinking—to make better sense of seemingly difficult situations. I've learned that "stinkin' thinkin'" was preventing me from reaching my full potential and getting the most out of life. Furthermore, I've experienced the tremendous satisfaction that comes from proving irrational beliefs (that seemed so real before) are just plain *wrong.*

I went through about a thousand elastics! Now I carry a psychological two-by-four that I use to give myself a whack upside the head whenever I start to drift into irrational or counterproductive thinking.

Like so many mothers, Allison based her teachings on intuition, experience, and good old common sense.

The most important role of psychology, in my view, is to affirm common sense. Research tends to follow the behaviour. For me, that's what the research of Martin Seligman, author of *Learned Optimism*, and more recently, *Authentic Happiness*, did. Seligman's theory of optimism goes something like this: People become optimistic or pessimistic depending on how they learn to explain events to themselves. We each have an *explanatory style* we use to talk to ourselves about setbacks and successes. Our explanatory style has three dimensions: permanence, pervasiveness, and personalization. Each affects our tendency toward optimism or pessimism.

Pessimists think setbacks are permanent; they use language like, "There will never be any work out there," or "Training will never help," to underline their belief that bad things will be permanent. Optimists, on the other hand, generally think setbacks are temporary problems, and will explain their beliefs with statements like, "The economy's not doing well right now," and "That sure was a lousy training course."

When it comes to successes, simply reverse the explanations of the pessimist and optimist! A pessimist attributes success to luck, extra effort, or some other temporary cause; an optimist, however, explains accomplishments with statements like, "I sure am good at this," or "I have a real talent."

Making setbacks and successes *universal* or *specific* is what the pervasiveness dimension is all about. Pessimists describe setbacks in universal terms ("I'm not smart," "I can't get along with people"), while optimists tend to use specific descriptions ("I'm not very good at math," "I can't get along with John Doe").

When it comes to successes, the explanations are reversed! Optimists believe their successes are universal (e.g., "I'm smart," "I get along with people") while pessimists think they are specific (e.g., "I'm good at science," "I sure get along well with John Doe").

Personalization has to do with the extent to which one regards the source of the setback or success to be internal or external. Pessimists internalize their set-backs by saying "I'm clumsy," "I'm a loser," while optimists externalize them: "My team has trouble working together," "My training was terrible."

As with the other two dimensions, the explanations are reversed for successes. Pessimists externalize, saying, "We won because the other team played poorly," or "That sure was an easy test"; whereas optimists internalize: "Our hard work paid off," "I was well prepared for that test."

Becoming optimistic, according to Seligman, is a matter of changing one's explanatory style—how one explains setbacks and successes. The essence of his approach is that our emotional and behavioural reaction (the *consequence)* has less to do with the *adversity* than the *belief* we have about the adversity.

Here's an example: a friend of mine has been an avid cyclist for years. He's ridden to and from work since long before the days of designated bicycle paths, on an old ten speed with a carrier over the back wheels that he uses to carry his lunch, rain jacket, clothes for work, and so on. Very ingenious idea, in my view.

He usually avoids the bicycle paths, and rides the city streets because, even though somewhat harrowing, he finds it quicker. The last leg of his ride into work is downhill for about three-quarters of a mile. One morning, as he was cruising down the hill, a car pulled around him. The driver was honking his horn and pointing at my friend in a seemingly less-than-friendly manner. Taking it as a case of road rage, my friend shook his fist back and loudly yelled, "Jerk!"

The car pulled into a gas station lot at the bottom of the hill, and the driver got out and stood next to his vehicle. *Probably wants to duke it out with me*, my friend thought. *Jerk! Well, bring it on. I'll let him know in no uncertain terms what I think of his stupid behaviour.*

Loaded for bear, my friend pedaled up to the car, prepared for battle. Before he could open his mouth, however, the driver handed him his rain jacket. "I thought you might need this," he said. "It fell out of your carrier at the top of the hill, and I was able to stop and pick it up."

My friend was tongue-tied!

The *adversity* was getting honked at, and the driver shaking his fist. For my friend, the *consequences* were the feeling of anger and the behaviour of yelling. His actual belief was something like "That rude jerk! He wants to run me off the road, and now he wants to do battle with me!" When the driver presented the rain jacket and my friend realized the true nature of his intentions, the consequence instantly changed. He didn't yell, and, by his own admission, felt somewhat stupid about getting so angry.

What's changed here? The *belief* about *adversity*! The belief controlled the consequence; the adversity did not.

According to Seligman, the secret to becoming optimistic is to work on beliefs that come between adversity (or good events) and the consequence, and aligning them with the appropriate poles on the permanence, pervasiveness, and personalization continua by using a five-step model as simple as A,B,C,D,E.

You already know about Adversity, Belief (that which drives our reaction and behaviour), and Consequence (the actual behaviour). What's new here is Disputation disputing the unhelpful beliefs), and Energization (the energizing consequences of disputing the unhelpful beliefs).

Here's how it works.

SCENARIO ONE

Adversity:	Gail, a small-business consultant, responds to a request for proposals, but her proposal is rejected.
Belief:	Gail's self-talk is: "I am terrible at writing proposals; I should never have tried consulting. I should just quit and start looking for a job."
Consequence:	Gail gets discouraged, quits responding to requests for proposals, and her business shrivels and dies.

SCENARIO TWO

Adversity: Gail, a small-business consultant, responds to a request for proposals, but her proposal is rejected.

Belief: Gail's self-talk is, "I am terrible at writing proposals; I should never have tried consulting. I should just quit and start looking for a job."

Consequence: Gail gets discouraged, but this time decided to dispute her negative beliefs.

Disputation: "I'm not really that bad at writing proposals. If I were, I'd never have gotten any business. They were probably looking for something outside my skill set. I think I'll check with the client and find out where I came up short, so I can prepare better next time."

Energization: Gail feels motivated, checks with the client, determines what she needs to increase her chances for success next time, and signs up for a workshop to improve her skills.

Notice the difference in Gail's energy and will to act when she disputes the negative beliefs. The more she disputes negative beliefs, the better she will become at it. In time, the disputation will become almost automatic as the energizing consequences of it reward her for the effort. Eventually, as it did with me, the positive explanatory style will become her "default" response.

People truly have one of two words written in their heart. The word of the optimist is *yes;* the word of the pessimist is *no.* Gail is on her way to becoming a yea-sayer rather than a nay-sayer—someone charged with positive energy, ready to take risks for a better life and maybe even a better world.

The difference between optimism and pessimism is far greater than a debate over whether the glass is half- empty or half-full; it has direct bearing on our chances for success, happiness, and long life. While optimistic people live longer, are generally healthier, and enjoy greater success than their pessimistic counterparts, they pay a price—because they are wrong more often than pessimists. But they have more fun.

Missing the net more often than hitting it is the   price of optimism—is the price too high, or is it a bargain? I think it's a bargain at twice the price!

> *To achieve the impossible, you must believe in the possible.*
> *to believe something is possible creates energy.*
> *To believe that something is impossible depletes it.*
> —Norman Cousins

A BIT OF AN EPILOGUE:

If all of this seems to you to be some oversimplified pop-psychology puffery, I want you to consider the story of Bill Porter.

Born with cerebral palsy at a time when society sent a clear message that people with that condition couldn't hope for any level of success or independence, Porter, encouraged by his mother, disputed those negative beliefs, substituted his own positive set, and became a door-to-door salesman selling household products for the Watkins Company in Portland, Oregon.

Friendly, persistent, and quietly optimistic, in time Porter became the top-grossing Watkins salesman in the United States. A widely reprinted 1995 column about Porter in *The Oregonian* made Porter a popular symbol of optimistic determination. *Reader's Digest* and the ABC newsmagazine *20/20* featured stories about Porter. In 2002, TNT cable made his life story into a movie called *Door-to-Door,* with actor William H. Macy portraying Porter.

Another thing to consider: Martin Seligman believes there is a powerful connection between pessimistic personalities and clinical depression—not just pessimistic in outlook during depression, but pessimistic before the onset of depression. According to him, pessimists are four to eight times more likely to succumb to depression. Further, he has developed a set of tools for diagnosing pessimistic personalities in people not yet diagnosed as depressed, and uses the techniques of learned optimism for dispelling the pessimistic cloud—changing their word from *no* to *yes.*

Chapter Nine

you don't marry the person you marry

*My husband and I have
never considered divorce... murder
sometimes, but never divorce.*
—Dr. Joyce Brothers

I t has been said that love is blind; love has also been
described as temporary insanity.

I think it's both—and that's a good thing. I mean, it's not
blind *forever*—actually, as you get older, you realize that it's
just a little myopic. But when you're younger, it really is blind.
And the insanity is temporary—it's cured by marriage.

Why are these good, then? Because, if you could see
clearly and you mind wasn't temporarily muddled, you might
never get married. And if you never get married, you never
learn the art of battle—not vicious or cruel battle, but good,
healthy, objective, honest, and constructive battle. Artful
lovemaking and romance may bring you together and get you
through the honeymoon, but believe it or not, battling artfully
is what keeps you together in the long term.

Someone once said that you don't marry the person you marry. If that's true, then whom *do* you marry?

Well, initially, it's the total stranger who shows up about two weeks after you say "I do." You know: the one with, among other things, a whole set of strange ideas about cleanliness, how to squeeze the toothpaste, why manners really count, what defines financial responsibility, and whose family you should spend Christmas with. "Where," you ask yourself, "did this strange person come from? And why didn't I see this coming?" Because love is blind, and you were temporarily insane!

Love and romance illuminate what we have in common—those shared behaviours, qualities, values, interests, and desires that attract us to each other and create the chemistry that causes us to become starry eyed and marriage-minded. But just as they do all those wonderful things, love and romance hide our respective flaws, annoyances, and differences. And if love is truly blind, it is to these things that it is blind.

So, we don't see—or choose to overlook—all that our prospective spouse is as a single person—all those weird behaviours, petty annoyances, and sloppy habits. And guess what? He or she is as a single person what he or she will be as a married person—only more so! The annoyances intensify after marriage because your spouse no longer has to worry about scaring you off— you've committed yourself to him or her!

And so what do you do? You begin put together a strategy to change your spouse into something better, something more like you; the irony is that your spouse is doing exactly the same thing, and so the battle begins! With any luck, it will continue for years and years. My wife and I have been lucky—we've been artfully battling for more than thirty years, and I hope we can keep it up for another thirty!

Contrary to popular belief, opposites do not attract. Think about it for a second. If you are a wild, crazy, ebullient person, do you seek out quiet, introspective people? I think not—you tend to seek out others who are more like you—people with whom you have characteristics in common. That was certainly the case for my wife and I. We're both extroverted, people oriented, fun, optimistic, trusting, democratic and collegial. We're both "high talkers," share a similar sense of humour and irreverence, and given an audience and opportunity, have a tendency to "entertain." Those and several other shared characteristics were the source of our mutual attraction, formed the basis for our premarital relationship, and provided the rationale for getting married.

Now, we didn't just set sail on the old sea of matrimony without some thought. Before getting in the boat, we looked for some navigational help. Among many other things, we went to premarital classes, talked at length with married couples we knew, watched "Who's Afraid of Virginia Woolf?"—exercises that I think are actually meant to help you realize that the ship of matrimony is at best a pretty tippy canoe, and at worst, a really leaky boat!

But love, lust, the opportunity to dress in some wonderful wedding finery, along with the allure of a great party and a pile of wedding presents precluded our seeing through the veil of romance and into the future.

And so, on August 10, straight out of university— three weeks before we were each to start our first teaching jobs— we got married, broke the champagne over the bow, and set out on the good ship *Tom & Marce*, anticipating nothing but fresh winds and clear sailing.

We didn't hit the shoals until August 11! It began at breakfast, when my new wife asked me how much money I had. "Thirty-two dollars," I said, "before I pay for breakfast." (Remember, this was 1968.)

"No, *really*," she said. "How much do you have?"

"Thirty-two dollars," I said.

She nearly went into cardiac arrest! "We're going on a honeymoon! How're we going to pay for it?"

"Credit card," said I.

It started with a low, guttural sound—kind of like a big dog's deliberate, menacing growl—and rose slowly until it reached the pitch and proportion of a primal scream: "Aaarrrggghhhhhh!" said my lovely bride of six-teen hours.

Now, I'm a fairly perceptive guy; on the basis of her less-than-eloquent response to the size of my bankroll, and a couple of unprintable references to my lack of general and fiscal intelligence, I quickly determined that her security needs were higher than mine!

That was the first indication that some of our "inner juices" were different. As it turned out, I was mixing yellow bile with blood, and I was doing it without a helmet! Inner juices? Yellow bile and blood? Yuck—I'd better explain.

Inner juices, or humors, are terms the Grecian forebears of Freud used to describe the "temperaments" that influenced human behaviour. Using really disgusting terms, a person was assigned to one of four types according to his or her predominant "humor," or "inner juice." Yellow bile made for a *choleric* temperament characterized by strong will, dominance, and self-confidence. Blood made for a *sanguine* temperament, producing a person who was optimistic, vain, and unpredictable. Phlegm created the *phlegmatic* character— slow but persevering, while black bile made a *melancholic*— reflective, solitary, and softhearted.

While my wife and I shared many of the sanguine characteristics, she also tended to be somewhat phlegmatic, while I incorporated a lot of yellow bile with my blood. In other words, while we were similar in many respects, in some others we approached life's issues from exactly *opposite* points of view! For example, where my wife preferred predictable, routine, steady situations that changed little from day-to-day, month-to-month, I was a change seeker, always dissatisfied with the status quo. I didn't know that until August 11!

The bile, blood and phlegm references—now thankfully out of fashion—were shorthand terms used to describe what we now call social or behavioural style— a person's predictable and preferred way of doing things. Today, just as in Grecian times, each of us has our own preferred approach to communicating, managing, motivating, decision-making, and influencing. And because this preferred approach generally works so well for us, we come to think that not only is it the best way to do things, it is the *only* way!

Nothing could be further from the truth. As often as it supports us, our preferred approach gets in the way, because, more often than not, we're dealing with someone else whose needs and behavioural styles differ from our own. That person may not share, understand, or appreciate our motives and approach.

What do we do? How do we minimize the reaction that results from mixing blood and bile?

The first step is to increase awareness of behavioural styles and their impact. Awareness of your own personal style, as well as the styles of others, helps provide better understanding of the strengths and shortcomings of the various approaches—and, in the end, enables the choice of behaviours more appropriate to the situation at hand. This, in turn, creates outcomes that are more satisfactory for everyone involved.

There are many instruments and programs that provide insights into behavioural style. The needs based DISC framework is one of my favourites. Leveraging off the theories outlined in William Moulton Marston's book, *The Emotions of*

Normal People, the **DISC** structure defines four behavioural tendencies: *Dominance*, which describes those who seek to control their environments through direct action; *Influencing*, which describes people who tend to persuade others to work with them; *Steadiness,* types who work to cooperate with others in a steady, consistent manner; and *Cautious*, people who work within existing circumstances to provide quality and accuracy.

The theory behind DISC is fairly straightforward: needs determine goals, and goals motivate behaviour. That is, if we have control needs, we consciously or unconsciously establish goals concerned with achieving control, and then we behave in ways that help us achieve those goals. Different people have different needs —hence, different goals, and different behavioural approaches. We are motivated, then, to behave in ways that will lead to achievement of our own goals, rather than the goals of others.

Going back to our second day of marital bliss for a minute—once my wife had apprised me of her high security needs, she went about explaining the types of behaviour that would be required to fulfill those needs: prudent, stable, careful, low-risk, no credit cards, and so on. She then told me unequivocally that these were the types of behaviour she expected from me as a dutiful husband. Well, *that* wasn't going to happen, at least in the near term, because my needs for security were so limited. I didn't even know how to be prudent, stable, careful, low-risk, how to operate without credit cards, and the rest. Actually, I suggested, perhaps it would be better if *her* behaviour could reflect a somewhat higher tolerance for risk and change—a little closer to the edge, if you like. That wasn't going to happen, either— at least, not in the near term.

Of course, each of us thought we were right! And so it began. And on it's gone, for more than thirty years. Each year, I might add, has been better than the previous one. How did we survive the differences? By getting rid of any notions of entitlement we had—by recognizing we had no right to a happy marriage, only the opportunity to create one. And, as with any opportunity, it was going to require a lot more work than luck.

We realized we were going to have to examine and align our values. We determined we needed to recognize, accept, and celebrate our differences, and use them to create the synergies that would help us move forward. We accepted that a certain amount of risk taking was going to be involved. We came to terms with the notion that dissonance, rather than comfort, was the stuff of progress. We recognized we needed to learn how to communicate with each other, how to resolve conflicts in ways that satisfied us both, and how to create a culture of success.

We had formed a long-term partnership, one within which we each had roles to play and jobs to do. The extent to which we dedicated and committed ourselves to making the partnership work would determine the degree of success it enjoyed. Although the romance was still present and important, it wouldn't sustain the marriage. The honeymoon was over, and now the real work needed to begin.

If you're beginning to see some emerging parallels between marriage and careers here, you're right! Just as we don't marry the person we marry, we rarely end up doing the job we were hired to do. And those nice people at the interview turn out to be much different than they appeared to be when they presented the offer. There's a honeymoon period after which the bloom comes off the rose and we're actually expected to make a contribution and produce some results (the biggest difference between marriage and work I suppose, is that you don't get to sleep with your co-workers!). Further, much of what's needed for either a successful marriage or successful career is remarkably similar.

Aligned values, for instance. *Do Values Matter?* Absolutely! Values provide the foundation upon which your needs, goals, decisions, and actions rest. They are the rules by which you run your life. If your behaviour is seriously out of sync with your own values, those of your partner, or those of your employer, you risk disharmony, conflict, and chaos.

Whether consciously or unconsciously, we rank values in order of importance, and then work to satisfy them in that order. For example, if you value power above all else, before pursuing any other value, you will align your behaviour with that value by consciously or unconsciously making decisions and engaging in behaviours that satisfy your need for power.

Because values can change throughout life, value clarification and alignment can be an ongoing process. And because, in the words of Socrates, "the unexamined life is not worth living," we should revisit our values on a regular basis. (A bit of a disclaimer, here. Appropriate examination of life is healthy, but over-examination is not only counterproductive, it can turn one into an insufferable bore. People who make an almost full-time job of navel-gazing or spiritual searching are generally self-indulgent, self-involved and tedious people. In contrast, those who spend less time in self-examination and who get involved with other people are more interesting because they have more interesting selves to examine.)

So, how do you revisit *your* values?

Decide whether you want to focus on work or your personal life. Once you've decided on the context, do a little "internal brainstorming." Generate and write down as many words as you can think of that describe what you believe and value—keep asking, "What's important to me? What else is important?"

Once you've exhausted your thinking, circle the words that jump out as being the most important. You'll probably find six to twenty words that qualify as value descriptors. Write these on a separate sheet of paper, and then create a hierarchal list by ranking them in order of importance. You've now identified and ranked your values.

When you've finished, compare your list with your employer's values, or those of your spouse or partner, and identify areas of alignment and conflict. Develop and implement strategies, to strengthen and reinforce areas of alignment, and reduce or eliminate conflicts.

Engaging in this exercise helped me realize that my values precluded me from having a career in public education. It helped my wife to realize that what she valued was inconsistent with working outside the home. As a couple, it enabled us to recognize and analyze the gaps, and create strategies for dealing with them.

Improved business success, improved customer relations and satisfaction, increased leadership skills, improved teamwork and innovation, improved morale, and heightened job satisfaction are among the many benefits of clarifying and aligning values. But not all values will align, and that's a good thing, because acting from a position of sameness and complete agreement is a little like drinking your own bathwater—you can live on it for a while, but eventually the poisons in it will kill you.

To move forward requires a dissonance and discomfort—some dissatisfaction with the status quo, and a notion that there is a better way. In the words of Scott Peck,

The truth is that our finest moments are most likely to occur when we are feeling deeply uncomfortable, unhappy, or

unfulfilled. For it is only in such moments, propelled by our discomfort, that we are likely to step out of our ruts and start searching for different ways or truer answers.

It was forever thus. Were this not the truth, I suspect we would still be living in caves.

So there's a need to change, to get out of our comfort zone, recognize, accept, and celebrate differences, and use them to create the synergies that would help us move forward. Who makes the first move? You do!

I can hear you saying, "Why me? Why am I the one who has to change? Why can't the other person or other people change for me?"

Well, most simply, you have be the one who changes because the other person probably won't. You can wish, hope, pray, bleed a chicken, do a ritualistic dance on the coffee table, or mutter some ancient incantation in backward Latin, but it's still not likely the other person will change. You'd like to control the other's behaviour, but you can't. So, you control what you can control, and the only variable you control in an interpersonal situation is *your own behaviour.*

Regardless of whether you are dealing with personal or work-related difficulties, there are only four choices: *change yourself, change the elements of the situation, learn to live with them, or terminate the relationship.*

Now I won't claim for a minute that I haven't considered the latter choice on occasion, especially during the early years of our marriage. But whenever the idea came up, I'd remember my father's advice: "You'd better not leave something unless you've got something a lot better to replace it with." I can honestly say I've not seen anything better, so that left the other three choices. And the first one, change yourself, is the best one.

What do you do, then? You challenge your beliefs about adversity, revisit your values, alter your goals, and, from a behavioural perspective, you become versatile and adaptable. You adapt your behaviour, according to what's happening and the needs of the person you're dealing with. You avoid the treat-others-as-you-want-to-be-treated Golden Rule, and adopt the Platinum Rule: *"Treat others as they need to be treated."* You work to create win-win outcomes.

While many refer to win-win in terms of objective outcomes, such as "expanding the pie," or "restructuring the deal," my sense is that people's feelings about how you expanded the pie are more important than who got what. In other words, psychological rather than objective outcomes decide whether you achieve a win-win solution.

To that end, win-win, then, is about dealing with differences from a cooperative rather than an adversarial perspective, and, in the end, it's about accomplishing what's important to you while, at the same time, meeting the needs of others.

Where do we start? By using a communication approach that promotes achievement of Francis of Assisi's plea, "Grant that I might not seek to be under-stood as to understand."

Ask.

Listen.

Respond.

In that order.

What do you ask? Questions that look for answers to:

"How do you see the problem?"

"What will happen if we don't solve it?"

"What do you need from me?"

Questions like, *"What's happening here?"* *"How long has it been going on?"* *"How do you see all of this; what's your interpretation?"* *"What elements of the current situation are causing difficulty?"* *"Functionally, what cannot be done unless we make some changes?"* not only imply interest in the other person's views, they help you get to the root of the other person's thinking. If he or she is defensive or resistant, it helps you to discover the source of the resistance, and if you can do that, you can take steps to reduce it. Reducing resistance is a much more effective way to bring disagreements to resolution than applying force.

"What effects does this have on your ability to...?" and *"How will that affect your people/your emotional or physical state?"* address the importance of the issue. This type of questioning helps you to discover the importance placed on the issue by the other person, and discover what perceived benefits resolution might bring. Essentially, these questions help you to discover what the other person needs.

As you get answers to these questions, use supportive body language, listen actively, and paraphrase important facts. Pay attention to the meaning implied by body language and tone of voice. Move the conversation forward, by asking clarifying questions and probing for deeper understanding. Launder the language by taking out volatile phrases or language. Reframe issues, focusing on the interests, not positions. Be forward thinking—focus on the future.

All of this is in the name of letting the other person know you understand where they are coming from, and their feelings about what's happening—getting you on the "same page" and speaking the same language, if you like. Once you're satisfied that your understanding of the other person's issues and interests is as complete as possible, you can do what everybody is tempted to do first; respond or offer your solutions.

Couch your response in the form of a question, such as *"What do you need from me?" "Do you think that this will work?" "If we did this, would it alleviate the situation?"* The answers to these questions will confirm the value or usefulness of your proposed solution.

The principal advantage of doing all of this is that, if you are true to the process, whatever you propose has a greater chance of meeting the other person's needs and providing the benefit he or she is looking for. And if you can give others what they need, there is a higher likelihood that they will give you what you need.

This is a very portable process. You can use it for sales, negotiation, solving people-problems, building consensus around decisions, and conflict resolution.

Can you create win-win solutions in every case? Probably not—in fact, in where time is limited or simple compliance is enough, there is no need to go through the process. But if quality and buy-in are important, you're well advised to go through the steps.

And, whether in your personal or professional life, when you get the buy-in and are ready to move on, there are a few ideas to keep in mind. First, remember that if people know what's expected of them, that's what they'll do—if they don't know what's expected, they'll do something else. Communicate clear and unambiguous performance expectations, and hold people accountable for their achievement. This is true whether you are dealing with children, colleagues, spouses, or those who report to you.

Be a systems thinker. Remind people of their inter-connectedness, and that something happening in one area affects all other areas. If people know how what they do impacts on others, they'll try harder to do it well.

Keep people informed. Don't assume that others can read your mind. If there's something going on, let them in on it. Without information, people invent it, and the human tendency is to think the worst. A well-timed word can prevent a lot of worry.

Remember your first car and how you felt about owning it, and how hard you worked to keep it clean and in good running order? Well, the same holds true for people's jobs. If people feel ownership of their job, the harder they will try to take care of it and do it well.

Establish a feedback culture, both at work and in your personal life. Things go wrong probably no more than five or ten percent of the time, yet we spend ninety percent of our time belabouring those few things. We probably only spend ten percent of our energy talking about the ninety percent of things that are well done. Spending more time providing feedback about the positive outcomes makes it easier to talk to people about those that are negative.

Passing on a good word about someone or providing deserved praise or recognition doesn't diminish you in any way. It doesn't take any light from your candle to light someone else's. Feedback truly is the breakfast of champions, and people who feel like champions act like champions.

Invariably, when I ask those in my training sessions who has power in the room, they point to me. To an extent, that's true: I do have power, but only if they give it to me. And they can take it away as quickly and easily as they gave it. When someone gives us power, he or she expects that we will use it responsibly.

People who use power responsibly shun manipula-tion and intimidation, and focus on what they can give to others rather than on what they can get. They share their power, giving others the opportunity to influence events and situations. And, like the biblical direction about "casting your bread upon the waters," the return is a thousand-fold. Those with whom the power is shared give it back in greater measure, and the mutual ability to influence is enhanced. Simply put, power shared is power gained.

When a sports team performs poorly, the coach is fired, not the players. And the players, not the general manager, fire the coach. How does all of this work? Quite simply, the coach fails to provide the conditions that motivate players to maximize their performance, and as a result, they play just hard enough to keep their jobs. "Spoiled athletes," you might say. "The money they make should be enough to motivate them!" But money only keeps them coming back. Take it away, and they won't come at all; but more of it will do nothing to make them work or play harder.

Have you ever noticed how hard volunteers work, how dedicated most of them are, and how much time they give to their volunteer organizations? Why is that? Well, mostly because others recognize and appreciate their skills. Often their assignments are important jobs and carry large responsibility. Recognition and opportunity are what drive volunteers. Treat the people who work with you like volunteers, and the results will amaze you.

Finally, whether it's your spouse, your kids, or those who work with you, remember: what happens while you're there doesn't matter—it's what happens when you're not there that counts.

One of the great rhetorical questions of all time, in my view, is "How can I fly with the eagles when I have to work with the turkeys?" I'll bet you've heard that. Moreover, I'll bet that you've also *said it*, perhaps with some minor variation, but implying the same message.

The great curse of humanity is that we have to work and live with other human beings, however incredibly frustrating that may be.

When something goes wrong with a human being, there is rarely if ever a quick, easy fix, unlike when a computer or a copier goes wrong and we simply replace the faulty part with a new one. Human beings do not come with interchangeable parts.

In my training, I often use a behavioural model that identifies three fundamental skill areas— Technical, Human, and Strategic—as having varying degrees of relevance for people in the workplace. Essentially, the model shows that, as one progresses through the organizational hierarchy, his or her dependence on technical skills decreases, while the need for strategic skill increases. But regardless of where one is in the hierarchy, the need for human skills is constant. Effectiveness at any level requires abundant levels of emotional intelligence or "people skill."

The same holds true in our personal lives. While the need for certain types of skill will vary as we move through the various phases and stages of life, the need for emotional intelligence and interpersonal effectiveness remains constant. And we cannot give too much attention to that notion.

Every training program I do has a session on interpersonal effectiveness. And although the workshop participants may have been previously exposed to the ideas and skills, they respond as though it is all brand-new. Why? Because the people they're dealing with today are not the same people they dealt with yesterday. Oh, the faces may be the same, but each person is a little different today by virtue of the life and work experiences they've had since yesterday. They're different people, and because of that, you need fresh approaches to working and coexisting with them.

You don't marry the person you marry; you don't do the job you were hired to do; and you don't work with the people who hired you.

Marriage is that relation between man and woman
in which the independence is equal, the dependence
mutual, and the obligation reciprocal.
— Louis K. Anspacher

Tom Olson

Chapter Ten

pulling off an inside job

*A rut is a grave with
the ends knocked out.*
—Laurence Peter

Wanted: A few people lacking competence, energy, and drive, to do work that offers no challenge whatsoever. We will give those with limited backgrounds and bad attitudes preference. Don't even think about getting any recognition— we are an equal opportunity employer. No phone calls. If you can pull yourself together long enough, send your resume to the Human Resources Department, XYZ Company, 111-11 Avenue, Anywhere, USA.

Have you ever seen an advertisement like this one? I would hope not! Organizations don't hire people like those described in the ad, do they? No, they hire smart people, hard-working people with good attitudes. People like you and me. And we are smart.

Think about it for a minute. When you look at yourself in the mirror before going to work in the   morning, do you say, "Boy, am I ever a dolt! I don't know why I was ever hired. I have no education, experience, skills, or worthwhile background. I've never made any worth while contribution, and it's unlikely I ever will. I guess I'll just go into work and screw a few more things up..."?

No! What you say is actually more like "I'm capable, competent, and confident. I'm good at my job, and make a great contribution to my organization. I'm going to do the best job I can today." And, most of the time, you meet that objective, until, like many people, you begin to lose your zest for the job, and start to feel like the person described in the ad.

Over the years, I've tested the notion of personal competence and confidence in my training sessions by asking individual participants the following: Are you the kind of person:

- Who makes a significant difference?
- Who is generally self-directed?
- Who is creative and innovative?
- Who looks for and exploits opportunities?
- Who looks for the resources and competencies to exploit opportunities?
- Who is a good team builder and networker?
- Who is determined in the face of adversity and competition?
- Who can manage change and risk?
- Who puts the customer first?

Almost overwhelmingly, the answer to these questions is "Yes!" I then ask, "Would you like the opportunity to be all of these?" Again, the answer is overwhelmingly "Yes!" Unfortunately, however, the answer to the final question, "Are you give enough opportunity to be all these things?" is a resounding, unequivocal, "No!"

There, in my view, lies the reason people are "pulled" to self-employment. According to the HRDC and Statistics Canada (2000) Survey of Self Employment in Canada, nearly one Canadian worker out of six was self-employed in the year 2000, and roughly four out of five of these people were "pulled" into self-employment. That is, they became and remained self-employed by choice, rather than because of downsizing or a lack of suitable paid employment opportunities. In my view, almost every one of these people represents a significant loss to the companies from which they were "pulled."

Data generated by the same study pointed out that people are "pulled" into self-employment because they want independence, freedom, the chance to be their own boss, better balance between work and family life, flexible hours, and greater challenge, creativity, success, and satisfaction in their working lives. Also, the desire to earn more income, and to have more control and responsibility in the workplace pulls people to self-employment—all of those things they weren't getting at work.

And how do they feel about what they are getting now? University of Alberta professor Karen Hughes, along with Grant Schellenberg and Graham Lowe, has developed a useful way of measuring job quality and satisfaction. For their research into "Men and Women's Quality of Work in the New Economy," done for the Canadian Policy Research Networks, they articulated the idea of "Job Quality Deficit." This is a measure of the difference between what people want in a job, and what they *have* in a job—essentially, the gap between the ideal and the reality. The larger the deficit, the more the job falls short of expectations. The smaller the deficit, the closer the job is to one's ideal work situation.

They used the Job Quality Deficit measure to find out if the self-employed actually have smaller job quality deficits than employees. They examined several job dimensions, including communication (working with friendly and helpful people, and having good communication with colleagues or clients), intrinsic rewards (the opportunity for interesting work, training, skill development, and accomplishment), psychological attachment (one's work commitment and involvement, a sense of shared values and respect), and work-family balance (the ability to choose one's schedule, balance work and family, and have some influence on one's working life). In a nutshell, the researchers found that, on each of these job dimensions, the percentage of people who have large job quality deficits is considerably lower among the self-employed.

So... does this mean I think everyone should leave his or her job and become self-employed? By all means, no! Although there are many compelling reasons for going out on your own, most people are simply not willing to take the risk. What I *am* suggesting, however, is you can reduce whatever job quality deficit you might currently feel by making your job more like self-employment.

"And how," you ask, "am I supposed to do that?"

Well, I don't think you can do it alone. You're going to need the help of your boss and others in the organization. But it does start with you. You start by deciding what you want to be known for in your organization.

Do you want to be known as one who:
- Has a kaleidoscopic view of the company, constantly looking at it from different angles and seeing resources combined in different ways to address different needs?
- Sees everything as variable, nothing as fixed, and assumptions as existing only to be challenged?
- Understands possible futures and creates the future of his or her choice?

- Is regarded as one who asks the good questions rather than just the safe ones?
- Would rather ask for forgiveness than for permission?
- Wants your colleagues to think of you as an intra-organizational revolutionary who challenges the status quo and fights to change the system from within?
- Finds a ready source of "free" resources within your company that can be used to move the company in a different direction?
- Do you want to be acknowledged as an individual who is good at seeing patterns of change?
- Is renowned for the ability to see failure as a temporary setback, an investment in education, and, most importantly, an opportunity to learn and to do better next time?
- Is thought of as the type who thinks that you should do something about what you think is wrong?

Or would you like to be considered a slug-like drone with no interest in anything beyond showing up, standing upright, breathing through your nose, and collecting a paycheque?

Answering "yes" to any or all of the above (except for the last one, of course) may qualify you as an *intrapreneur*—one of those people described by Gifford Pinchot in his 1987 article, "Innovation Through Intrapreneuring," as *dreamers who do.*

If you tend to be independent and visionary, have good communication skills, a high sense of curiosity and self-worth, like to feel a degree of ownership of your work, are willing to take risks, make decisions, and take responsibility willingly, you definitely qualify.

An intrapreneur is a paid employee who asks, *"What if?"* and then, using assertive risk-taking, creativity, and innovation, answers the question by producing a profitable finished product, process, or service. Does the intrapreneurial creation always have be something large or earth-shattering? Not to my mind. All it needs to do is alter the relationship between effort and outcome, so you get more of the latter with less of the former!

To do that, you have to challenge the status quo— change the elements of the situation so they better meet your needs. Be unreasonable, and follow the dictum of George Bernard Shaw, who wrote,

The reasonable man adapts himself to the world;
the unreasonable one persists in trying to adapt
the world to himself. Therefore all progress
depends on the unreasonable man.

(George was thinking great thoughts long before the notion of inclusive language became popular.)

Challenging the status quo requires three things:

1. *Innovation*—the ability to see things in novel ways.
2. *Calculated risk-taking*—the ability to take calculated chances, and to embrace failure as a learning experience.
3. *Creativity*—the ability to conceive of multiple possible futures, and to proactively create the one you most need.

An ancient Chinese curse says: "May you live in interesting times." These are interesting times, indeed. Phenomena such as globalization, outsourcing, technology, and staffing have sparked massive changes in how we do work and operate business. As the pace of change quickens, organizations are finding that last year's ideas and solutions are no longer applicable to today's challenges.

Companies are asking employees at all levels to find solutions that offer something new, something different, something... creative. In the words of Edward DeBono,

As competition intensifies, the need for creative thinking increases. It is no longer enough to do the same thing better... no longer enough to be efficient and solve problems. Organizations need much more. Now business has to keep up with changes... And that requires creativity. That means creativity both at a strategic level and on the front line, to accom-pany the shift that competitive business demands... from administration to true entrepreneurship.

So, you need to be creative. But, if you're like most people, you probably think of creativity as the exclusive province of artists, musicians, actors, and writers. From within your own paradigm, you likely see creativity at work as something too difficult to define, and even harder to implement. Perhaps it's time to smash that paradigm and replace it with a new and different view of creativity and creative action.

Often, before I start a workshop, I suggest that I'm not going to teach anything new—just remind the participants of what they already know, and help them rearrange that knowledge so they can use it more effectively. My notion of creativity is much the same. To me, it is not really a process of inventing something new; rather, it is a process of unwrapping and repackaging current information, energy, and resources to find new ways to act, solve problems, or link ideas, processes, or procedures.

In short, creativity is uncovering, selecting, rearranging, and synthesizing your own inventory of facts, ideas, and skills to produce results that are novel, useful, and predictable. It is the act of awakening new thoughts—of rearranging old learning, and of examining assumptions to form new theories, new paradigms, and new awareness.

What, then, is stopping you? Perhaps the greatest barrier to creativity is a reluctance to look past acceptable or easy models of behaviour and thinking—like the man who lost his keys one night in a dark alley, but walked around and around the corner street lamp looking for them, "because the light is better here."

Creativity is looking where the light isn't.

Some of the barriers that keep you looking only where the light is are:

- Getting stuck on one "right" answer to a problem.
- Conforming to established patterns and resisting change.
- Believing that outside forces are in charge
- Lacking confidence in our own ideas and opinions
- Allowing others to judge what's "right" or "wrong"
- Being afraid of looking like fools
- Making premature or uninformed judgments.

So, how can you "uncover what is already there," or "look where the light isn't"? You take creative action.

There are several ways to do this. First, there is *innovation*, or an original approach to a problem. Innovation involves seeing the obvious before anyone else does.

Second, there is *synthesis,* or combining existing ideas from various sources into a new whole—bus companies offering courier services, for example.

Third, *extension* involves expanding an idea to another application. A number of different businesses— including banking, dry cleaning, and, as I have been told, New Orleans liquor stores—extended the fast-food restaurant "drive-through" idea to create new opportunities and successes for themselves.

Fourth, there is *duplication*, the simple form of creative thought that involves simply copying others' good ideas—General Motors developing a "retro"look car after Chrysler's success with its PT Cruiser, for instance.

Now bear with me while I engage in a little creative activity, and try to create an acronym that incorporates all these approaches to allow you to be more C.R.E.A.T.I.V.E. Here goes—use the following verbs to force your thinking to go in different directions when thinking about how to improve a product, service, or process:

COMBINE—can we make this product/ service/process more effective by combining it with something else?

REDUCE—can making this product/ service/process smaller, or doing less of it, increase its effectiveness?

ELIMINATE—could we do without this product/service/process altogether?

ADAPT—can an adaptation of another product/service/process create more effectiveness?

TURN IT AROUND—can we increase the effectiveness of this product/service/process if we reversed, rearranged, or otherwise turned it around?

INCREASE—can we add value to this product/service/process by making it bigger, or doing more of it?

VARY—can we increase effectiveness if we put this product/service/process to another use, or vary the way in which we use it?

EXCHANGE—could we add value to this product/service /process by exchanging parts of it with something else, or all of it for something else?

How's that for an acronym?

This approach is but one among many. There are any number of books, tapes, and courses available for those interested in learning more. Regardless of the approach you take, keep the following in mind to increase the effectiveness of your creative efforts.

- When you're generating ideas, concentrate on quantity first. Collect all the ideas you can, and jettison the bad or unworkable ones later.
- There is rarely, if ever, just one right answer or one right way to do something.
- If most people tell you that your idea will never work, you're probably on the right track. If you hear hoots of derision, you're *definitely* on the right track!
- A lot of failure usually precedes a little success.
- Overnight success is a myth.
- There are no dumb questions.

- Keep a pad and pen handy to write down ideas before you forget them—especially those that come in the middle of the night!
- The need for new ideas is near, not in the distant future.
- From the minute you get an idea, picture how things are going to look after you implement it.
- Replicate and extend.

There is little question that creative and innovative thinking and action will contribute to your intrapreneurial efforts, regardless of how grand or limited you intend them to be.

Be forewarned, however —built into most organizations, yours included, is a "corporate immunesystem" that acts as a form of creativity retardant by smothering new ideas as quickly as you introduce them. If the costs of failure are higher than the rewards for success, if there is inertia caused by organizational systems that nobody is willing to change, or if the organization is bureaucratic and hierarchal, the corporate immunity will be exceptionally strong.

If the immune system in your organization is too overwhelming, you may have to abide by the intra-preneurial rule about keeping your ideas underground, and working subversively until you can show them to be viable. Working underground is one of the many risks associated with intrapreneurial thought and action. You need to ask yourself what risks you are willing to take to bring your ideas forward, and how you will manage these risks.

Being creative or acting in an intrapreneurial way puts you at risk of, among other things, ridicule, failure, loss of face, demotion, conflict, losing credit, rejection, even being fired. But if you want to help create greater customer value, more openness, new systems, better management, different incentives, greater creativity, more collaboration, clearer vision, less bureaucracy, flatter structure, different culture, less resistance to change, better teams, more efficiencies, better teamwork, more flexibility, and more tolerance for mistakes, these are probably risks worth taking.

Aside from taking and managing risks, you need to determine which boundaries (job description, personality, learning style, organizational values and culture, personal thoughts and beliefs, family and organizational expectations) you're ready to cross, as well as what changes in yourself (level of risk tolerance, behavioural style, assertiveness, work style) you're willing to be accountable for.

Finally, you need to do a personal skills inventory and decide what you'll need to be successful.

Next steps?

To paraphrase JFK, "Ask not what your company can do for you, ask what you can do for your company." Learn more about your company, and how it does what it does. Look for opportunities to cross-train. Find a mentor and/or sponsor. Ask lots of questions and listen to all the answers. Don't be afraid to either discuss contentious issues or disagree. Share both your gratitude and successes with your mentor. Get as many people involved in your ideas as you can. People are stronger supporters of what they help generate or create.

Become a lifelong learner. Read, listen, take classes, and seek input from both customers and outsiders. Always regard criticism as an opportunity to learn how to do things better. Operate in the short term, but think long term.

And, finally, remember the intrapreneurial com-mandment that you should come to work each day willing to be fired. (When I had real jobs, I used to come to work expecting to be fired!) I know what you're thinking: "Come willing to be fired? That makes no sense at all!" In fact, it does, and there's more security in coming to work willing to be fired than there is in coming to work, doing your job, and hoping that it won't disappear through some form of reorganization or at the whim of a new vice-president.

It takes courage to play the intrapreneurial role— the courage to do what's right, rather than the right thing. It takes a lot of courage to let go of the familiar and ostensibly secure, and embrace something different. Something that is no longer meaningful, however, is not really secure. As most entrepreneurs and intrapreneurs find, there is more security in the new, adventurous, and exciting. And they would almost unanimously agree that in movement, there is life, and in change, there is power. You can't achieve your goals if you lack confidence or are fearful.

Why were you hired in the first place? Because you're smart, capable, competent, and confident. That knowledge alone should give you the courage to challenge the status quo and make things better. And if you're producing results, should your boss ever be foolish enough to fire you, you'd have another job in no time.

But only if you produce!

So, if you feel you have a large job quality deficit, take off your helmet and go for it!

We do not believe in ourselves until someone
reveals that deep inside us is something valuable,
worth listening to, worthy of our trust, sacred to
our touch. Once we believe in ourselves we can
risk curiosity, wonder, spontaneous delight or
any experience that reveals the human spirit.
—e.e. cummings

Tom Olson

Chapter Eleven

weasel, toad, slippery, and puke

*Security is mostly a superstition. It does
not exist in nature, nor do the children of men
as a whole experience it. Avoiding danger is
no safer in the long run than outright exposure.
Life is either a daring adventure or nothing.*
—Helen Keller

When I was in high school, the guidance counselors scheduled annual appointments with students according to the first letter of their surname. My appointment was always in late March. I have no clue why they adopted this system, but it must have worked for someone.

Looking at it from our perch in the twenty-first century, it does seem a patently silly system, doesn't it? I mean, it seems to assume a correlation between one's last name and when problems associated with teenage angst are going to take hold. So, it was all right to be angstridden, just as long as it happened during your assigned month—if your surname begins with "W," don't even *think* about having a problem until the late spring!

None of us really cared, though. Not that we didn't have problems—we just weren't sure why and how we should involve a guidance counselor with them. The purpose and inner workings of the guidance department were a complete mystery to most of us.

The guidance counselors themselves were usually members of the physical education faculty who, in the final analysis, provided neither guidance nor counselling! What they did do was show up in health classes to lecture about dating etiquette, the dangers of smoking, dancing too closely, or the dangers of smoking *while* dancing too closely. These lectures were usually accompanied by out-of-date, jerky black-and-white movies with questionable soundtracks and bad acting. Usually, when the lights went down, a bunch of people would sneak out to dance and have a smoke.

At least once each year, the counselors would divide us along gender lines, and herd the boys into one room and the young women into another, and give us the annual "naughty bits" lecture. Always a highlight of the year, these lectures invariably began with the guidance counselor, whom I suspect had less experience with the "naughty bits" than many of my classmates, warning us in hushed, conspiratorial tones that "nothing said here today leaves this room." Then, in the most awkward, inadequate, and uncomfortable way, he would try to fill us in on the sweet mysteries of life.

When he ran into problems or was unable to answer a question, he would defer to Jim Read. Jim was fifteen and knew more about the nuts and bolts of the naughty bits than Hugh Hefner. He would answer questions for the teacher until the bell rang. The counselor would heave a sigh of relief, thank Jim for his contribution, and dismiss the class.

Jim, whose dad had the world's largest collection of *Playboy* magazines stashed in his basement, would invite us over to his house to carry on the discussion. We went en masse. I think the guidance counselor wanted to accompany us, but was afraid to ask.

Such was the state of guidance counselling when I showed up for my annual appointment in March of eleventh grade. In the previous year, I had completed an aptitude survey. It was quickly scored, and the conclusion was drawn that I had a future either in tree surgery or horse grooming. I expected that this visit would be more of the same. To my surprise, instead of a test, I got some advice—or maybe it was counselling.

"Olson," the counselor started, "I think you should quit school now, and go out and get a low-paying service industry job before the qualifications needed to get them go up."

Thank God he was a trained professional—I can't imagine how he might have delivered that message had he not been trained!

Now admittedly, I was not the best student in the school, but I didn't think I was *that* bad. I mean, I was passing some of my courses, had only been suspended three or four times in two years, and was on track to graduate before my twentieth birthday. I was being treated unfairly, and my self-esteem (although I didn't know that's what it was at the time) was suffering. I reacted with considerable umbrage, fixed the phys-ed-guy-turned-counselor with a steely gaze, stood up, and said, "Wait until my dad hears about this!"

I turned and left, confident that my father, upon hearing how I'd been treated, would immediately march down to the school and set things right. He'd let that counselor know that I should be recognized as the rocket scientist I really was. Furthermore, if there were any more assaults on my self-esteem, he would tell the school officials to expect a call from his lawyer!

When I told him what happened, however, my father sided with the school!

He told me he agreed with the counselor's assessment that I'd been causing the school more trouble than I was worth, and it probably *was* time to quit and get a job. "You wouldn't be in this position if you'd paid attention, done your homework, and studied for exams," he said. "You created this mess, and now you have to clean it up!"

A parent siding with the school—imagine that. After dinner, needing to commiserate with someone I thought would be more in tune with my cause, I got my unhelmeted body on my bicycle and rode off in search of my four best friends— Weasel, Toad, Slippery, and Puke. These weren't their real names, of course. They were nicknames tacked onto each because of some physical characteristic or unfortunate public accident. Slippery was so named because of his excessive use of hair oil; Weasel, because he bore a startling likeness to the creature of the same name; Toad, because he had warts; and Puke—well, *you* figure it out.

Everybody, even the teachers, knew these guys by their nicknames. I would go so far as to say that their real names were unknown to most. Even today, many years later, old friends still greet them by these same monikers.

How they must have suffered from these insensitive labels—how hard it must have been on their respective senses of self. I really don't know how they survived the teenage years, much less adulthood, with the weight of these derogatory nicknames resting on their shoulders.

Today, Puke is a senior partner in one of the largest law firms in the country; Slippery is the president of a publicly traded oil-service company; Toad is a dermatologist, and

Weasel is an accountant. Man, they must have had a lot of counselling!

In any case, I found my four amigos standing in front of Fobert's Grocery, sharing a soft drink. They had pooled their money and come up with just enough cash for one Coke, and were passing the bottle around when I arrived. I grabbed it and had a quick swig, thereby adding a fifth set of DNA to the rim of the bottle.

How disgusting and dangerous was that? I'm surprised any of us lived after having shared all that potentially life-threatening bacteria. We must have been just plain lucky, because in the summer we always drank water directly from the garden hose—and that didn't do us in, either.

I told them about my experience with the counselor and my dad's reaction. They pretty well agreed that I was wrong, and the counselor and my dad were both right. Then, if as to punish me for both my lack of perception and being the smallest of the group, they collectively threw me to the ground and pummeled me mercilessly for about ten minutes. Actually, we took turns pummeling each other—it was something we did on a pretty regular basis.

Man, talk about peer abuse and bullying—those guys should have been given some sensitivity training, and I probably should have had some counselling so I could deal better with the trauma of getting about twenty noogies and six wedgies in a public place. A little Ritalin probably wouldn't have hurt, either—it would have calmed them down and quelled their unacceptable behaviour.

Having grown tired of heaping verbal and physical indignities on each other, we repaired to the park across the street to play a little dodge ball and plot our strategy for the upcoming weekend. Boy, did that ball do a job on Weasel's nose—I didn't think it was ever going to stop bleeding. After a close examination, the consensus was that it hadn't been broken—a big disappointment for the Weasel. A broken nose would gotten him out of school for a few days, and given him something to talk about for months.

Funny, his parents didn't sue our parents and us. I guess they just thought it was one of those accidents that kids have growing up.

No one was really to blame.

Imagine that.

Anyway, once the blood from Weasel's nose slowed to a trickle, we put together our plan for Saturday. We decided to spend all day ice fishing at Alan Beach. Although spring had just arrived, we were sure that the ice would still be safe to walk on. We made a list of the stuff we would need, and agreed to meet early Saturday morning. All helmetless, we jumped on our bikes and rode home through the gathering darkness.

When I arrived home, my mother was putting my niece, who was with us for a "sleep over" to bed in my old crib. We had recently painted the crib with a bright, lead-based yellow paint, and she was happily chewing on the one of the rails as my mother was tucking her in.

I wonder how come my niece didn't glow in the dark or something when she got older? In fact, why didn't I— I had slept in the same crib, except then it was blue. More blind luck, I guess.

I filled my Mom in on the evening, and let her know about our plans for ice fishing on Saturday.

"That's nice, dear," she said. "How are you going to get out to the lake?"

"Hitchhike," I replied.

"That's nice, dear," she said again.

I went to the kitchen to get an Aspirin, and make myself a snack to tide me over until my bedtime snack. I pulled the cotton out of the Aspirin bottle, got an Aspirin, popped it into my mouth, and washed it down with some water straight from the faucet. My mom kept the Aspirin and some other patent medications in a cupboard next to the sink. They were always accessible—no childproof lids or devices on medicine bottles, doors, or cabinets. *When I think about it, it's amazing nothing untoward ever resulted from that lack of precaution.* Well, not unless you count my brother's unfortunate experiment with the chocolate flavoured laxative. Now, *that* was messy! He got a pretty neat nickname out of it, though.

Having swallowed my Aspirin, I then proceeded to devour a white Wonder Bread peanut butter-and-jelly sandwich, three carrot-cake muffins with cream cheese icing, and a Cherry Coke. I was skinny as a whippet, had the metabolism of a wolverine—but still, all that sugar, fat, and white flour! If I hadn't spent so much time outside riding my bike, playing baseball, hockey, dodge ball, and just about any other sport you could name, I probably would have been huge—maybe even obese.

You know, I think I missed an opportunity. I could have sued the food manufacturers for millions, and retired to a life of leisure without even graduating from high school. What were my parents thinking, letting me do all that athletic stuff?

Still a little hungry, but not wanting to spoil my late night snack, I shuffled into the living room and flopped down on the sofa to watch *The Untouchables*. Even before Elliot Ness had confronted the first Capone mobster, my father came into the room and flipped off the television. "How many times have I told you that you can't watch this stuff? It's too violent!" he muttered.

I guess he was an early version of the chip that those interested in controlling what their children watch can now install. "But what am I supposed to do?" I asked. "We only have two channels, this one and the CBC, and who wants to watch *Front Page Challenge?* "

"Go read," he said.

I picked up a book by Jack London. I read until I couldn't keep my eyes open. What a story. I could just imagine White Fang and the pit bull, the arguments, the fights—who knew that reading could be that much fun? Of course, the light was bad, and I was probably in danger of straining my eyes.

How could my father, in all conscience, expose me to that risk? Plus, all the main characters in the book were men—how was I ever going to learn about the important role played by women during the Yukon gold rush?

The next couple of days passed quickly, and before I knew it, Saturday morning had arrived. I got out of bed, had three or four bowls of sugared cereal for breakfast, used an entire loaf of Wonder Bread to make peanut butter-and-jelly sandwiches for lunch, packed my fish filleting knife and Sterno Stove, and set off to meet the guys at Toad's house.

I rang the bell, and Mrs. Toad hollered for me to come in. Toad and his family were just finishing breakfast and asked me to join them, which I happily did. The downside was that they were having waffles with maple syrup and bacon. I never really liked waffles, but I had twelve to be polite. The arrival of the rest of the guys coincided with my swallowing the last waffle. We checked our equipment, said goodbye to Mr. and Mrs. Toad, and made our way to the highway.

Now, five guys hitchhiking can be difficult, especially when one is carrying an ice auger. Very few people were willing to provide a ride for a crowd like that, but we were lucky—within a couple of minutes, a guy driving an old Chevy pickup pulled over. He was going to the same place as we were, so we hopped in—two in the cab, and the other three back in the box.

The pickup had a four-on-the-floor that made it a little crowded, to be sure. Luckily, there were no seat belts to deal with, so we could shuffle around to make more room when he had to shift gears.

You know, when I think about it, we did this all the time: took rides with total strangers, rode in cars with no seatbelts or airbags, and had ourselves ferried around in the beds of pickup trucks. Geez Louise, it's a wonder we survived. Blind luck, I guess.

What a day we had! Slippery was the only one to fall through the ice, but that was close to shore, and it happened after we'd finished fishing, so no real harm was done. We hung his wet pants over the fire, and then, using my knife, started to fillet the perch we'd caught through the ice. Toad cut his finger, but we had bandages. We rolled the fillets in flour, fired up the Sterno, threw about half a pound of butter in a frying pan, and cooked up fifty or more fish. We ate until we could eat no more, and then, just to stay in practice, pounded on one another for fifteen or twenty minutes.

After the ritual noogies and wedgies, we laid on our backs, looked at the clouds, and talked about how lucky we were. We were free! Our parents knew where we were, but there was no way that, short of actually driving out to the lake, they could get hold of us. No cell phones—*imagine that.*

We talked until late in the afternoon and then, reluctantly, packed up our stuff and walked to the highway to hitch a ride home. We weren't lucky enough to get a ride home in a pickup, but did get a lift in a brand-new Buick driven by a cigar-smoking fat guy who told us ribald stories all the way back to the city. He dropped us right in front of Puke's house. We thanked him for the ride, punched one another a couple of times for good measure, and promised to meet at the park after church the next day.

Church? How weird was that—I mean, was it really healthy to have all that patriarchal, biblical, moral absolutism foisted on kids, giving them ideas about right and wrong? Shouldn't that have been balanced with some teachings about Wicca, Eastern Mysticism, and the God within? Geez, it's a wonder we turned out as normal as we did!

When I went back to school on Monday, the counselor told me that if I wanted to stay, I'd have to perform better—if I didn't perform, I was out. Regardless of what I did, he told me I had no chance of graduating with my friends—I'd have to wait until a year later. And, unless I received passing grades, I couldn't walk the stage at graduation, and couldn't attend any of the ceremonial stuff.

My God, how draconian! Didn't these people realize how leaving me behind would cause me personal suffering, poor self-esteem, and lifelong scarring? However, I learned something about the relationship between actions and outcomes.

I stayed behind, and I haven't had to go to one counselling session. Blind luck, I guess.

Later in the week, the coach cut Weasel, Slippery, and me from the rugby team. Our dads didn't call the coach, or threaten to sue the rugby association. The three of us learned to live with it.

Some of the best risk-takers and problem solvers and inventors ever were products of the generation that spawned my friends and me: a generation that contributed a veritable explosion of innovation and new ideas. We had freedom, failure, success, and responsibility, and we learned how to deal with it all. We did it without the interference of that ever-expanding cadre of bureaucrats and counselors who, for the past twenty-five years or so, have created and perpetuated the belief that people cannot cope on their own.

We did it without the burgeoning counselling industry, the relentless emphasis on boosting 'self-esteem', and the expansion of syndromes, disorders and traumas that encompass more and more life events. We did it without today's obsession with 'the fragility of internal life'—that sense that people can no longer judge themselves based on their achievements in society, or their relationships with others.

Now, don't think for a minute I'm suggesting that we can return to the carefree existence of my youth. We can't. For better or worse, the world is a different place, and there are some very real issues that should concern us. But I do think we need to put these into perspective and deal more rationally with our almost-pervasive culture of fear. The sky is not falling—you *can* leave the house.

Here are a couple of statistics from the National Safety Council about the chances of your dying in some accident or disastrous event. They are:

- 1 in 1,500,000 of a terrorist-caused shopping mall disaster, assuming one such incident a week and that you shop two hours a week;
- 1 in 55,000,000 in a terrorist-caused plane disaster, assuming one such incident a month and that you fly once a month.

In his wonderfully written book, *The Culture of Fear: Why Americans are Afraid of the Wrong Things*, Barry Glassner reminds us again and again that often our fears about teen-mother tragedies, rare diseases, youth crimes, and airplane crashes are grossly exaggerated, given the actual frequency of these rare events. It's a worthwhile addition to anybody's library.

Why is it necessary to gain a perspective on all of this? Because our belief, perhaps obsession, with food scares, abuse, stranger danger, disease and impending environmental disaster serves to diminish our roleas agents of our own destiny, and lowers our collective expectations of what we can get out of life. The unsubstantiated risks we supposedly face, and the inclination to believe the worst about the human condition not only diminishes us, but also works to create a bleak future for our children.

> *Fear is not the natural state of civilized people.*
> —Aung San Suu Kyi

references

We all have heroes and role models —people we admire and look up to; people who, in one way or another, instruct our lives in ways no amount of reading or formal study could. People who value what we value, and who consistently model behaviours we want to emulate. People whose personal definitions of success are congruent with ours, and whose lives serve as examples of how we should live our own.

I have many heroes and role models, and while some of these I know by reputation only, for the most part, they are friends, acquaintances, neighbours, and colleagues who have consciously chosen the *freedom* door, and have been successful on any number of levels. Let me introduce, in no particular order, some of them.

Jim Staples, Rita Popowich, Frank Kernick, Scobey Hartley, Jeff Sluggett, Georgie Clarke, Bev Durvin, Beverley Hatcher, Jim Mayhew, Jim Francis, Bill Aube, Bill Dalton, Jim Cleave, Susie Babani, Clive Beddoe, Albert Elliot, Barb Banman, Marcelo Olson, Bruce Brennan, Vince Ekvall, Chuck Blanchard, Brian Young, Jeff Dowle, Liz Pedersen, Larry Jurgens, Kenny Mayer, Billy Sumner, Erin Hyrniuk, Tawnie Olson, Pat McAllister, Gail Kench, Pat Pitsel, Diane Dutton, Bob Lane, Robert Haynes, Tim O'Shea, Glen Philips,

Harold Pedersen, Brad Trumble, Don Ross, Shaun Murphy, Diane Barker, Preston Manning, Daryl Banman, Kathy Sluggett, Lindsay Olson, Clayton Woitas, Peter Ford, Alan Neilsen, Earl McLaughlin, Jim Sadler, Spencer Fried, Joan Sumner, Harry Grant, Merla Pedersen, Roger LeBlanc, Rick Durvin, Gerry McAllister, Karen Bird, Ralph Klein, Tony Nicastro, Cam Waddell, Don Gass, Jim Kollee, Donna Young, Judy Philips, Linda Jurgens, Ryan Sluggett, Doug Hartley, Glen Popowich, Simon Wilson. Denny Coates, Meredith Bell, Marshall Stawart, Lynne Ross, Bob Schmitz, Stewart McNair, Ed Williams, Ron Robertson, Arthur Sheffield, Bob Somerville, Lorri Neilsen, David Scobey, Darwin Gillies, Connie Artym-Bradatsch, Grey Bradatsch, Brian Crookes, Rick Durvin, David Wood, Fran and Nelly Hubbard, Chuck Ross, Kurt Pedersen, Dr. Atkins, June LeBlanc, Neil Mackeith, Bill Baker, Carrie McLaughlin, Roberta Barker, Therese Grant, Shannon Gillies, Butch Bishop, Jan Campbell, June Mackeith, Nita Staples, Uncle Bern, Jack Frost, Wende Brash, Gavin Bird, Deb Skaret, Bob Harris, Michael Appleby, Jason Roe, Don Fraser, Gary LaPointe, Dean Loewen, Bill Sykes, Josh Woitas, Stephen Harper, Ezra Levant, Elizabeth Nickson, Colby Cosh, Wynne Chisholm, Rob Anders, Dave Rutherford, Bill Winn, David Maxwell, Catherine Cook, Ron Clements, Roberta Hutton, Gerry Taft, Ron Parks, Jack and Anita Vossepoel, Jaime Brash and Roy MacGregor.

suggested reading

Byrd, Jacqueline, and Lockwood, Paul.
    *The Innovation Equation: Building Creativity and
    Risk-Taking in Your Organization.*
    Brown John Wiley & Sons, 2002.

Covey, Stephen R.
    Seven Habits Of Highly Effective People.
    1st ed. Simon & Schuster, 1990.

DeBono, E.
    The Five-Day Course in Thinking.
    The New American Library, 1967.

Furedi, Frank.
    *Culture of Fear: Risk Taking and the Morality of
    Low Expectations.*
    Cassell, 1997.

Furedi, Frank.
    *Therapy Culture: Cultivating Vulnerability in an
    Uncertain Age.*
    Routledge, 2003.

HRDC and Statistics Canada (2000).
    "Survey of Self-Employment in Canada."

Glassner, Barry.
  *The Culture of Fear: Why Americans Are Afraid of
  the Wrong Things.*
  Basic Books, 2000.

Hansen, Mark Victor, and Allen, Robert G.
  *The One Minute Millionaire: The Enlightened
  Way to Wealth.*
  Harmony Books, 2002.

Hughes, Karen, with Grant Schellenberg and Graham Lowe.
  *"Men and Women's Quality of Work in the
  New Economy,"*
  Canadian Policy Research Networks. Sept. 2003.

Kouzes, J ames M., and Posner, Barry Z.
  The Leadership Challenge, Third Edition.
  3rd ed. Jossey-Bass, 2003.

Kuhn. R., ed.
  Handbook for Creative and Innovative Managers.
  McGraw Hill, 1988.

Michalko, M. Thinkertoys:
  A Handbook of Business reativity for the 1990s.
  Ten Speed Press, 1991.

Peters, T.
  Thriving on Chaos.
  Knopf, 1989.
Pinchot, Gifford.
  "Innovation Through Intrapreneuring,"
  Research Management, March-April 1987.
  Volume XXX, No. 2.

Seligman, Martin.
> *Authentic Happiness: Using the New Positive Psychology to Realize Your Potential for Lasting Fulfillment.*
> Free Press. (September 4, 2002).

Seligman, Martin.
> *Learned Optimism: How to Change Your Mind and Your Life.*
> Reissue ed. Simon & Schuster, March 1998.

Senge P.M.
> *The Fifth Discipline.*
> Doubleday, 1992.

Thompson, C.
> *What a Great Idea.*
> Harper Collins, 1992.

VanGundy, A.B.
> *Idea Power: Techniques and Resources to Unleash the Creativity in Your Organization.*
> Amacom, 1992.

Von Oech, R.
> *A Whack on the Side of the Head: How to Unlock your Mind for Innovation.*
> Warner Books, 1983.

ISBN 142511216-1

9 781425 112165